ALTERNATIVE MEDICINE

ALTERNATIVE MEDICINE

THOMAS J. BILLITTERI

Twenty-First Century Medical Library
Twenty-First Century Books
Brookfield, Connecticut

To my parents,
Mathew and Pauline Billitteri

Photographs courtesy of Peter Arnold, Inc.: pp. 15
(© Still Pictures/Edwards), 28 (© Walter H. Hodge), 31
(© Ed Reschke); PhotoEdit: pp. 18 (© Mark Richards), 58
(© Michael Newman), 81 (© A. Ramey); Photo Researchers,
Inc.: pp. 29 (© 1998 Alan & Linda Detrick), 38 (© Hattie
Young/SPL), 77 (© Will & Demi McIntyre), 89 (© Jeff
Greenberg); The Image Works: p. 74 (© Dick Blume)

Library of Congress Cataloging-in-Publication Data
Billitteri, Thomas J.
Alternative medicine / Thomas J. Billitteri.
p. cm. — (Twenty-first century medical library)
Includes bibliographical references and index.
ISBN 0-7613-0965-9 (lib. bdg.)
1. Alternative medicine—Juvenile literature. [1. Alternative
medicine.] I. Title. II. Series.
R733 .B554 2001 615.5—dc21 00-057707

Published by Twenty-First Century Books
A Division of The Millbrook Press, Inc.
2 Old New Milford Road
Brookfield, Connecticut 06804
www.millbrookpress.com

CONTENTS

ALTERNATIVE MEDICINE

INTRODUCTION

In this book, you will read about a fast-growing method of health care called alternative—or complementary—medicine. Alternative medicine is a different kind of care than you may be used to receiving from your family physician or local emergency clinic. It uses such therapies as herbs, acupuncture, hypnosis, and special diets to try to heal people or help them stay healthy. Alternative medicine has helped many patients, but it also has limits and, in some cases, dangers. None of the information in this book is meant as advice for a specific medical problem. And readers are cautioned not to try the therapies mentioned without the guidance of medical professionals. The goal of this book is to help you become a wise consumer of this emerging field of medicine.

More than 500 types of alternative medicine exist, and thousands of treatment approaches are possible.

While this book does not attempt to address them all, it includes discussions of many popular kinds of alternative therapies. Chapter 2 focuses on herbal and dietary therapies, along with several broad systems of alternative medical treatment that include herbal therapies in their treatment approaches. Chapter 3 focuses on therapies that use the mind, spiritual activities, and the subconscious in an attempt to heal. Chapter 4 focuses on treatments that use bodily stimulation, such as massage and acupuncture, or so-called energy-based therapy such as therapeutic touch. The final chapter looks at the future of alternative medicine.

Included are ten hypothetical cases that represent a composite of circumstances in which alternative-medicine techniques might be considered.

Chapter One

WHAT IS ALTERNATIVE MEDICINE?

Andy's Story

For weeks, Andy hadn't been feeling right. During a getaway visit to his beach house, he noticed a vague sensation of bloating in his abdomen. By the time he returned to work on Monday, his stomach hurt. Andy's job as a lawyer had been stressful in recent months, and at first he thought he might simply have had a touch of indigestion from working late and not eating right. But Andy vomited after dinner twice the following week, and soon after that he noticed he was losing weight.

Andy consulted his family physician, and a series of tests confirmed the doctor's suspicions: Andy had a peptic ulcer—a break in the lining of the digestive tract—accompanied by gastritis—an inflammation of the stomach lining.

11

Any number of things could have caused these problems or made them worse, including bacteria, stress, and poor diet.

Andy's doctor recommended that he take a prescription drug to cut down on the amount of acid his stomach was producing. That, in turn, would allow the ulcer to heal. Andy's doctor also recommended an antibiotic to kill any bacteria that may have been responsible for the ulcer. Finally, the doctor suggested that Andy adopt a fiber-rich, low-acid diet and consider taking a prescription tranquilizer to help alleviate his work-related stress.

Andy recognized that his ulcer was serious enough to demand medical attention. But before he took his doctor's advice he decided to check out another option. He had heard about an emerging trend in health care called alternative medicine, an approach that uses a variety of natural remedies such as herbs, relaxation techniques, and acupuncture to bring about healing. Never a fan of prescription drugs, Andy decided to consult a friend, Maria, a specialist in alternative medicine, to get her advice on his problem.

Maria, a doctor trained in naturopathy, or natural medicine, and a licensed acupuncturist, reviewed Andy's test results and had a long talk with him about his lifestyle, diet, work, and personal background. As a naturopath, Maria believes that the body has the power to heal itself, and that its natural state is one of physical and mental equilibrium. When that equilibrium is disrupted, as it was in Andy's case, it is important to find out the underlying causes. That is what Maria was trying to discover.

After learning more about Andy, Maria rec-ommended a combination of alternative thera pies. Her advice was designed to reduce the acidity in Andy's digestive tract, heal the diges-tive tissue, and reduce the stress that Andy was feeling.

After making sure that Andy did not have high blood pressure, Maria suggested that he take licorice tablets to increase the mucus lining in his digestive tract. She also recommended a powder made from slippery elm, an herb native to North America, to reduce acidity and soothe the mucous membranes of Andy's stomach and intestines.

In addition, Maria told Andy that he could benefit from acupuncture treatments, in which a series of fine needles are inserted into strategic spots on the skin, producing favorable neural or chemical responses in the body. While acupunc-ture is often used to relieve pain, Maria thought it would help reduce the amount of acid that Andy's stomach was producing.

Maria also recommended that Andy adopt a fiber-rich diet and that he eat small, frequent meals to ease his stomach. Finally, she suggested that Andy consider undergoing hypnosis therapy—a procedure that can help people change harmful behavior patterns—as a way of helping him alter his stressful lifestyle.

Andy made no immediate decision about which course of therapy to adopt. He went home, thought it over carefully, and a few days later consulted with his regular medical doctor about the steps Maria had suggested. Once he felt he had all the information before him, he made his choice: He would adopt the diet rec-

ommended by both practitioners, take the antibiotic to eliminate any harmful bacteria in his system, try the herbal remedies that Maria had recommended to help heal his digestive system, and consider the hypnotherapy to help him manage the stress in his life. Andy rejected prescription tranquilizers, and he decided to wait before trying Maria's acupuncture remedy.

Most important, Andy made sure that both his medical doctor and Maria knew the details of all the treatment regimens he was following, an important step in avoiding complications or adverse physical reactions.

In a few weeks, Andy was feeling better, and a year after his bout with a peptic ulcer, the problem had not recurred.

Before there were hospitals, physicians, test tubes, or pharmacies, people turned to nature and folk traditions to stay healthy and to cure sickness. Native American and Eastern healers used herbs, shrubs, and tree bark to mend wounds, stop pain, and ward off disease. Some three thousand years ago the Chinese began practicing acupuncture. Shamans, or medicine men, throughout Asia, Africa, and the Americas diagnosed illness by observing the way people looked and acted, noting the color of their tongue, the pace of their heartbeat, their mood, and their dream patterns.

Such techniques may seem very strange in the modern world of gene therapy and fast-paced trauma centers. But the health practices of ancient civilizations are still with us today. Millions of people around the world continue to rely on herbal medicine, acupuncture, and other ancient remedies as their main form of health care.

Traditional healers the world over, like these in Cameroon preparing medicinal plants, have been practicing what Western medicine considers "alternative" medicine for centuries.

In recent years, a growing number of Americans have been turning to these ancient folk remedies to supplement—or in some cases replace—modern medicine. In addition, they are adopting controversial new treatments, such as magnetic-field therapy and commercial diet supplements, that are not endorsed by mainstream medical practice or prescribed by most family doctors.

Taken together, these treatments—ancient and new—have come to be known as "alternative" or "unconventional" medicine. Sometimes they are called "complementary" or "integrative" medicine, because people often combine these therapies with the care they receive from their regular doctor or clinic.

Alternative medicine has been attracting a growing number of American consumers. A 1990 survey of more than 1,500 American adults, published in the *New England Journal of Medicine*, found that 34 percent of respondents had used at least one alternative therapy in the previous year. Topping the list were relaxation techniques (used by 13 percent of respondents) and chiropractic medicine (10 percent), followed by such treatments as spiritual healing (4 percent), herbal medicine (3 percent), and hypnosis (1 percent).[1] A survey of more than 2,000 adults that was published in late 1998 in the *Journal of the American Medical Association* estimated that 46 percent of Americans had visited an alternative medicine practitioner in 1997, compared with 36 percent in 1990.[2]

In recent years, U.S. medical schools have begun studying herbal remedies, acupuncture, and other alternative treatments, using strict scientific methods to evaluate their safety and effectiveness. Some schools are also teaching certain alternative techniques to students studying to be doctors. In addition, the National Institutes of Health opened the National Center for Complementary and Alternative Medicine to help evaluate treatments, raising scholarly interest in the subject.

Alternative medicine shares a common goal with the kind of medicine most family doctors practice. But the philosophies and approaches of the two kinds of health care differ in important ways.

Conventional medicine is medicine that relies on modern research and technology. It is known as "Western" medicine because it was developed over many centuries mainly in the Western hemisphere—chiefly Europe and the United States. It is strictly regulated by the government, and its drugs and clinical procedures undergo rigorous scientific testing. Practitioners—called physicians, medical doctors, or M.D.s—must go through years of academic and clinical training before they can treat patients. Many doctors specialize in specific illnesses such as heart disease, cancer, or bone problems. They use synthetic drugs, surgery, and sophisticated machines to bring about healing. And while they try to help keep people from getting sick in the first place, most doctors focus on diagnosing and treating symptoms of people who are already ill.

Alternative medicine, on the other hand, is much more informal and freewheeling than conventional Western medicine. While some practitioners may have received rigorous training in their field, others may lack any professional credentials.

Alternative medicine's approach to healing differs from conventional medicine's too. It generally does not rely on surgery, sophisticated technology, or prescription drugs. Instead, it uses herbs, natural oils, massage, and spiritual methods among its techniques.

And unlike physicians, who tend to focus on symptoms in evaluating a patient, alternative practitioners often take a "holistic" approach. In other words, they take into account the patient's entire physical, mental, and spiritual status before diagnosing an illness or suggesting a remedy.

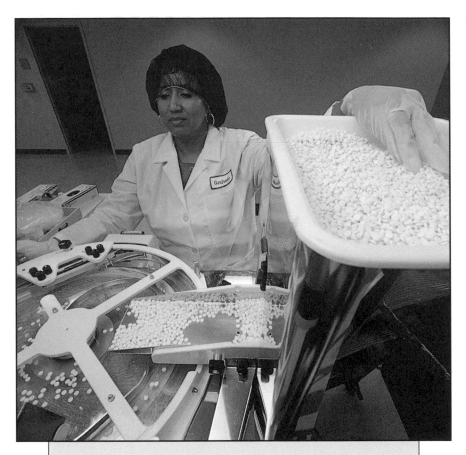

Conventional medicine generally relies on synthetic drugs to treat illnesses as they arise.

Finally, while most conventional doctors treat existing illnesses, alternative medicine puts as much emphasis on maintaining good health as on treating people who are already sick.

Experts in mainstream Western medicine have accepted some alternative treatments as safe and useful when practiced responsibly. For example, an independent panel of medical researchers concluded recently that acupuncture is an effective therapy for pain and nausea associated with certain medical conditions. Likewise, physicians often recommend vitamin supplements, massage therapy, or relaxation techniques such as yoga to their patients.

But many physicians and medical researchers remain highly skeptical of alternative therapy. They worry that people will bypass conventional medicine and choose unproven treatments, putting their health—and even their lives—at risk.

Even advocates of alternative medicine acknowledge that conventional treatments can be best in some circumstances. "If I have a car accident, don't take me to a herbalist," says Andrew Weil, a professor at the University of Arizona College of Medicine and a leading proponent of alternative treatments.[3]

Many alternative therapies are unregulated, and this can pose a danger. Drop by any pharmacy, health-food outlet, or grocery store these days, and you'll find shelves full of herbal remedies to treat everything from mild depression to insomnia to stomach ulcers. But what dosage is safe? Can an herb or vitamin supplement have side effects? And what happens if a patient combines herbal remedies with prescription drugs?

In fact, so many alternative treatments have entered the market since the early 1990s that researchers and consumer watchdog groups have not had time to check them all. (For examples of watchdog groups, see the Resources section at the end of this book.) Thus, *caveat emptor*—"buyer beware"—might be the best guide for the current alternative-medicine scene. Companies can market herbal supplements, for example, without having to prove that they are effective, as long as the wording on the package doesn't suggest that a product prevents, treats, or cures a disease.

Of course, any medical product or procedure—conventional or alternative—can be risky, and there is no guarantee it will work in every case. The best way to evaluate the promises and perils of alternative medicine is to know enough about individual treatments. In Chapter 2, you'll begin to learn about this emerging facet of American medicine, starting with one of the oldest therapies of all: herbal remedies.

Chapter Two

HERBAL MEDICINE, DIET, HOMEOPATHY, NATUROPATHIC MEDICINE

Ellen's Story

Ellen, 47, suffered from obesity and rheumatoid arthritis, and for three years she had been confined to a wheelchair. Always overweight, Ellen began to put on even more pounds when she was diagnosed with arthritis and it became harder and harder for her to get around. Her exercise regimen consisted of wheeling herself between her first-floor bedroom and her kitchen and, occasionally, through the corridors of a shopping mall near her home.

For several years, Ellen sought help from her family doctor, who prescribed increasing doses of prescription drugs for her arthritis. In the hope of losing weight, Ellen tried a string of crash diets and commercial weight-loss pro-

grams she read about in magazines. Her doctor tried to persuade her that such schemes were potentially harmful, but she ignored his advice.

Nothing seemed to work. Her arthritis grew worse, making it too painful for her to rise from bed or to dress herself some days. In addition, she suffered from the fatigue, fever, and joint swelling that often accompany severe rheumatoid arthritis.

Ellen also continued to gain weight. Because it was so painful for her to move, she was unable to exercise. She became depressed over her arthritis and obesity, causing her to eat more than ever. Prescription drugs to fight depression were available, but she resisted them, saying she preferred a "natural" approach to coping with her mood swings.

Ellen finally decided to seek the help of a licensed physician trained in alternative-medicine techniques. The physician recommended an herbal treatment, including wild yam, devil's claw, and nettle to reduce the symptoms of Ellen's arthritis. To combat her depression, the specialist suggested small—and temporary—doses of Saint-John's-wort. And finally, to reverse Ellen's obesity, the physician persuaded her to adopt a healthy, balanced diet that included ample quantities of fresh fruit, vegetables, and juices. He also got Ellen started on a regular exercise program.

In three months, Ellen was feeling much better. Though she still suffered painful bouts of arthritis, she was able to put away her wheelchair and take a part-time office job. She had lost twenty pounds and set a goal of losing *thirty more over the next year. And best of all, Ellen's gloomy outlook on life vanished, giving her the optimism she needed to cope with her arthritis.*

Belinda's Story

Belinda, a 39-year-old software executive, routinely had trouble falling asleep at night. In the past, she had turned to a prescription sedative or an over-the-counter sleeping pill to remedy the situation. But the sedative would leave her drowsy and listless the next day, and she worried about becoming addicted to the pills.

Belinda decided to try a new remedy for her sleepless nights: aromatherapy, the use of fragrances to create relaxing sensations or help with physical or mental healing.

She proceeded carefully with her desire to try aromatherapy. After reading about it and talking with her physician, she visited a shop that sold herbs and fragrances, and purchased an essential oil containing sandalwood, a balsamic aromatic that comes from the yellowish heartwood of a tree native to Asia. Sandalwood is sometimes used as an aphrodisiac, decongestant, or skin conditioner, but it also can help with nervous tension and insomnia, the clerk told Belinda.

Belinda added a few drops of sandalwood oil to the warm water of her bath and found the aroma relaxing. Soon after her bath she was asleep, and in the morning she was happy she'd avoided taking a pill to overcome her insomnia. Whether it was the warm bath, the psychological effect of trying a new remedy, or the subtle

*workings of aromatherapy that had helped,
Belinda didn't know. But she was intrigued.*

If you were a teenager in Europe a few hundred years
ago, you—like young people today—might have suffered from acne. But instead of taking antibiotics or
using special soap or cream, you might have been
treated with a concoction made with some of your vil-
lage's common plants, such as dandelion.

Herbal, or plant, remedies are among the oldest and
most frequently used forms of medicine. They are part
of a group of alternative treatments that also includes
nutritional supplements, fragrances, and special diets.
Often, small changes in the intake of nutrients or other
substances, perhaps coupled with carefully regulated
physical activity, can yield significant changes in a
person's health.

HERBAL MEDICINE

Herbal remedies, sometimes called "plant medicine,"
date back to the earliest civilizations.

The product of aromatic plants, herbs were used in
China more than three thousand years ago to treat
everything from headaches to problem pregnancies.
According to legend, the Emperor Shen Nung wrote
China's first compendium of herbal medicine, the *Pen
Tsao Ching (The Classic of Herbs)*, which listed hundreds of prescriptions using herbs. In the sixteenth century, Li Shih-Chen published a catalogue of medicinal
herbs listing thousands of formulas.[1]

Herbal medicine also took root in the West. In
medieval Europe, monks maintained herb gardens and
studied the medicinal uses of the plants, as did medicine
men among North American Indian tribes.

Herbs and other vegetation continue to play a strong role in modern medicine. About one-fourth of all prescription drugs are derived from herbs, trees, or other vegetation,[2] and a physician typically dispenses eight herb-based prescriptions each day.[3]

Herbs can be a leaf, stem, seed, or any other plant part. Some treatments call for herbs to be used whole. Other times, herbs are ground or rendered into an essential oil.

Herbs have natural chemicals, or active ingredients, that work inside the body much as pharmaceutical compounds do. But unlike some drugs that enter the bloodstream directly and affect the entire body, herbs tend to act on specific body systems. Often, they work slowly and gently, but not always. An herb taken in the wrong dose or form, or an herb of poor quality, can damage organs and even kill. For example, just a few tablespoons of oil derived from pennyroyal, used in other forms to treat cold and flu, can be fatal.[4]

In traditional Asian culture, herbs are used as part of a complex and mysterious system of medicine that takes a "holistic" approach to healing. That means it focuses not only on the physical aspect of a person's existence but also on the mental and spiritual.

Eastern thought views the mind, body, and spirit as a single system, bound together by an invisible force of vital energy called *chi* (pronounced "chee"). Sickness comes when opposing forces called yin and yang get out of balance and disrupt the flow of *chi*. Herbs, as well as other forms of alternative medicine, including acupuncture, help to move *chi* through the body along meridians—up, down, inward, and outward—and restore balance to the body.

Balance is also expressed in terms of five elements—earth, fire, water, wood, and metal. Each element is associated with plants having different tastes and medicinal qualities.

To treat a patient successfully, Eastern herbalists must assess thousands of plants for the correct substance, then determine the correct dosage and combination with other herbs. The task is difficult. Some herbs move a person's *chi* upward, toward the head, while others move it outward, making a person perspire (perhaps to sweat out a cold or expel toxins), or inward, to aid internal organs.

The theory behind herbal treatments can be bewildering. And yet, in recent years, many Western consumers have begun taking herbal supplements to address a wide range of health issues. Research on many herbal substances is under way, but scientists caution that the public's zest for herbs could be getting dangerously out of hand. In some cases, the safety and effectiveness of an herbal remedy depend on how the product is processed by the manufacturer and whether the herbs used are of good quality. Consumers must also be careful not to consume improper quantities of herbal remedies, or to mix them inappropriately with prescription drugs. In addition, many consumers fail to inform their doctors that they are taking herbal or dietary supplements, putting them at risk of dangerous interactions with conventional medical treatment.

Indeed, government regulation of herbal and dietary-supplement products is lax, putting both ill and healthy people at risk. Under the Dietary Supplement Health and Education Act of 1994, one consumer publication noted recently, "Congress largely deregulated the industry. The law assumes that since herbal remedies and body compounds are natural, they present few risks and don't need to be regulated as medicines. Instead, the law considers them in the food category and permits them to be sold over the counter as dietary supplements. But reports of the effect of some nutritional supplements on medical conditions suggest that they do, indeed, have druglike effects in the body. Interactions between some herbals and prescription medications are only now beginning to come to light."[5]

What's more, supplement manufacturers—unlike makers of prescription drugs—do not have to inform the government about the negative physical effects of their products.

Some herbalists are highly skilled, but some are not. Keep in mind that anyone can call himself or herself an "herbalist," "herbologist," or a "nutrition therapist" without passing any tests or meeting any government regulations.

Here are a few popular herbal remedies and some information on how they are used. This list is by no means exhaustive. But it will give you an idea of the uses of some of the products you may see on store shelves.

- **Ginseng.** One of the best-known Chinese herbs, ginseng has been used for thousands of years. People often take ginseng for physical and emotional stress, fatigue, fever, and insomnia. Advocates of ginseng say it also can bolster the immune system and help the liver function better. Ginseng is sold in various forms, including capsules, tablets, and powder. However, ginseng can produce serious side effects if taken for too long a period or in improper dosages. People with high blood pressure or heart problems should avoid the herb. Some experts warn against taking ginseng for more than a few weeks at a time.

- **Ginkgo Biloba Extract.** The ginkgo tree, native to China, is the only living species of a family of plants that were prevalent about 200 million years ago. The leaves of the ginkgo tree are used to treat circulation problems, brain injury, dizziness, asthma, heart, eye, and ear disorders, and other maladies. The Chinese prescribe the seeds to treat urinary and breathing problems. Ginkgo is especially popular in France and Germany, where people take it to improve memory and reduce the likelihood of stroke. However, an excessive dose could lead to serious physical reactions. Advocates believe ginkgo improves the memory of healthy people and reverses the mental problems resulting from Alzheimer's disease or stroke. But critics say there is no clear evidence of that.[6]

The leaves and fruit of the ginkgo biloba tree

The echinacea plant, commonly known as the coneflower

- **Echinacea.** A group of flowering plants native to the Great Plains region of North America, echinacea was a favorite of Native Americans. Research suggests that echinacea may help stimulate the immune system and lessen the symptoms of colds and flu. But the effectiveness of echinacea products may vary because there are different species and processing methods.[7] Critics fear that echinacea can depress the immune system, and they warn that people who are HIV positive or who have an autoimmune disease such as lupus or multiple sclerosis should avoid the herb.[8]

- **Garlic.** This pungent plant is used to treat a variety of ills, from colds and coughs to digestive disorders and high blood pressure. Consumed raw and in other forms, including capsules, tablets, and syrup, garlic is said to lower cholesterol and to relieve stomach and intestinal problems. However, a rigorous clinical study published in the *Journal of the American Medical Association* in 1998 concluded that garlic pills, a popular form of the herb, have no effect on lowering cholesterol levels.[9] Garlic can produce adverse side effects in some people, and it should not be administered as medicine to preteen children without first consulting a physician.

- **Saint-John's-wort.** Used medicinally for more than two thousand years, this herb is promoted in the United States and Europe as a natural remedy for depression. It got its name during the Middle Ages, perhaps because its flowers bloom in late June, when some Christians celebrate the birth of Saint John the Baptist. Scientists do not fully understand how Saint-John's-wort might work against depression. They speculate that compounds in the herb affect such brain chemicals as serotonin, promoting a feeling of well-being in people. Studies on mild depression have shown that Saint-John's-wort works as well as some prescription drugs and with fewer side effects.[10] But the reliability of the studies has been questioned, and a study reported in 2001 in the *Journal of the American Medical Association* found the herb to be useless in treating depression.[11] Moreover, cases have been reported in which the herb has had dangerous interactions with some prescription drugs.[12] Another study indicated that the plant might weaken the effectiveness of birth-control pills.[13] Other studies have found that Saint-John's-wort could interfere with drugs for heart-transplant patients and people infected with HIV.[14] The National Institutes of Health (NIH) has funded research to learn more about Saint-John's-wort.

Saint-John's-wort

- **Kava Kava.** Long used in the South Pacific for ceremonial and medicinal purposes, this member of the pepper family has been growing in popularity as a sedative and diuretic. It is frequently used for insomnia and stress and sometimes as a muscle relaxant. But experts say kava kava should be used carefully. It can produce intoxicating effects, and abuse of the herb can lead to skin rashes, blood damage, and other problems.
- **SAMe.** Pronounced "Sammy," this naturally occurring substance is neither an herb nor a hormone, but rather a molecule produced by living cells. SAMe is prescribed in more than a dozen countries for depression, arthritis, and liver disease, and it became widely available in the United States in the late 1990s. But SAMe has not undergone rigorous testing by the Food and Drug Administration, and some medical experts are wary of it.[15]

DIETARY SUPPLEMENTS

Alternative medicine also includes the use of nutritional and dietary supplements to help maintain or restore a person's health. Because the body does not manufacture some essential nutrients on its own, it is important to consume foods rich in those substances to stay healthy.

The Food and Nutrition Board was established in 1940 partly to set guidelines for adequate nutrition. Its list of Dietary Reference Intakes, which is updated periodically to reflect new scientific findings, estimates the nutritional needs of most people. But sometimes health-care specialists recommend supplements—to compensate for a deficient diet, to help people through periods of stress, pregnancy, or some other health-related circumstance, to ward off illness, or to compensate for the effects of aging.

Essential nutrients include proteins, which are made up of organic compounds called amino acids; vitamins and minerals such as calcium and iron; and fats and carbohydrates. Substances called cofactors work with the essential nutrients to help the body stay healthy. One example is the vitamin-B-complex compound choline, which helps to prevent excess fat from accumulating in the liver. The human body can make these substances on its own. But supplements can increase the amount of these compounds in the system.

Nutritional and dietary supplements are available over the counter at pharmacies or grocery stores, through the mail, through on-line vendors, or in some cases by prescription. They may come as pills or capsules, as creams or gels, in flakes, or in some other form.

A growing body of scientific research suggests that boosting the level of certain nutrients in the body may help protect against problems such as heart disease, infection, and osteoporosis—a softening of the bones that occurs with aging.

But it is important to take a common-sense approach to nutritional and dietary supplements. The mere claim that a product is "natural" does not make it healthy. Alcohol, nicotine, and the narcotic in cocaine, for example, are natural substances, but they can do great damage to a person's health.

You should also be aware that some nutritional and dietary supplements can cause great harm. Thus, large doses of vitamins A and D can damage the liver, and taking too much vitamin B_6 can lead to nerve problems.[16] In addition, excessive amounts of supplementary nutrients can interact with other nutrients in the body, canceling out their beneficial effects. For

33

example, too much calcium can lead to iron deficiency, and too much zinc can interfere with the absorption of copper in the body.[17]

One of the most controversial dietary supplements in recent years has been ephedra, which is derived from ma huang, a Chinese herb. Dietary-supplement companies promote ephedra as an energy stimulant or weight-loss product. The *Washington Post* reported in 2000 that dozens of lawsuits had been filed against makers of ephedra, blaming it for causing serious sickness or death.

"There is no agreement on what constitutes a 'safe dose' of ephedra," the newspaper said. In addition, it noted, the FDA had tried but failed to impose a dosage-labeling standard that would have been lower than the one that most companies had agreed to. The ephedra industry "successfully called the [FDA's] research into question," the *Post* said. "Under the 1994 Dietary Supplement Health and Education Act," it said, "ephedra products may be marketed without FDA screening, and are sold with almost no restrictions—much like vitamins or chewing gum." Without stronger federal rules on ephedra, some state and local governments imposed restrictions on the product's sales, the newspaper said, but "lawsuits may provoke the greatest changes in the industry."[18]

The controversy over ephedra serves as a warning that while some alternative treatments hold promise, others may have the potential to cause grave harm.

The bottom line: Eating right, taking a high-quality multiple vitamin each day, and, when it comes to nutrition, following the advice of a qualified physician or dietary specialist is the wisest approach to maintain health. Buying into trendy weight-loss diets, megavitamin therapies, or unsupported claims by herb promoters or makers of other controversial nutritional supplements without checking with an expert first can invite more problems than solutions.

AROMATHERAPY

This alternative technique uses essential oils rendered from herbs and flowers to treat everything from asthma and digestive disorders to menstrual troubles and skin eruptions.

The term "aromatherapy" is something of a misnomer because the oils are sometimes applied directly to the skin through massage or a warm bath rather than inhaled through the nasal passages.

Civilizations as ancient as the Mesopotamian, Egyptian, Greek, and Roman are said to have used therapeutic herbal oils that were rich in fragrance. Some writers credit the medieval Arabian physician Avicenna with developing a revolutionary way to distill aromatic oils from plants.[19]

The list of plants and fragrances used in aromatherapy is long; from lavender and rose to clary sage, chamomile, and lemon verbena. The essential oils rendered from such plants are mixed in highly diluted form with a medium such as sunflower oil.

According to aromatherapy theory, when the scent of an essential oil is inhaled, molecules in the oil stimulate the olfactory system in the nasal passages. The olfactory glands, in turn, interact with the brain's limbic system. The seat of emotional experience in the brain, the limbic system also controls such functions as heart rate, breathing, hormone production, memory, and breathing. The essential oils can have a direct psychological and physical effect, advocates argue. They say the oils ease respiratory disorders and other phys-

35

ical problems, alter a person's brain waves and mood, and help to regulate bodily functions such as blood pressure, metabolism, and stress levels.

When massaged directly on the skin, molecules of the essential oils are said to interact with the nervous system and, in some cases, directly with tissues that are in need of healing.

Skeptics say some claims of aromatherapy's healing powers far outpace available scientific research. Aromatherapy, they contend, may be little more than the power of suggestion at work. Many people associate specific smells with events or moods, the critics argue, so it is little wonder that a fragrance can affect a person's demeanor or physical well-being. But one aroma producing the same effect in a wide variety of people is doubtful, the critics say. After all, one person may have a pleasing memory of a fragrance such as lavender, while another person may associate it with an unpleasant experience.

Physicians in the United States seldom treat their patients with aromatherapy. But in France, researchers have long studied the subject, and doctors sometimes prescribe the essential oils instead of conventional drugs.

Like all alternative treatments, aromatherapy can have dangers. Some essential oils can be toxic if taken internally. And some can produce allergic reactions and inflammation of the skin.

HOMEOPATHY

The system of medical treatment known as homeopathy was founded by the German physician Samuel Hahnemann about two hundred years ago. Hahnemann was displeased with the standard medical practices of his day, which included bloodletting and the administration of dangerous toxins, such as mercury, to purge sick people of illness.

Homeopathy is based on the theory that small amounts of a medicine will treat a disease even though that same substance would produce symptoms of the disease if taken in larger doses by someone who is healthy. Two other principles guide homeopathy as well: that the effectiveness of homeopathic medicine increases as it is diluted, and that a single remedy should cover all symptoms, both physical and mental— a different approach from conventional treatment, which often uses separate medicines for each symptom.

"Some homeopathic remedies are so dilute, no molecules of the healing substance remain. Even with sophisticated technology now available, analytical chemists may find it difficult or impossible to identify any active ingredient. But the homeopathic belief is that the substance has left its imprint or spirit-like essence that stimulates the body to heal itself."[20]

Homeopathy is practiced throughout the world and is especially popular in England, France, Germany, India, and several other nations.[21] In the United States, millions of dollars in homeopathic drugs are sold each year.

At the turn of the twentieth century, 15 percent of U.S. physicians were homeopaths.[22] As medical science advanced throughout the century, homeopathy lost its popularity. But with the rise of alternative medicine in recent years, new attention has been focused on homeopathy in the United States and the United Kingdom.[23]

Whether homeopathic treatments work is a matter of debate within the medical and scientific communities. Advocates claim that homeopathy offers an effective alternative to antibiotics, is often the best approach for treating viral infections, and diminishes or does away with the need for some surgery, although hom-

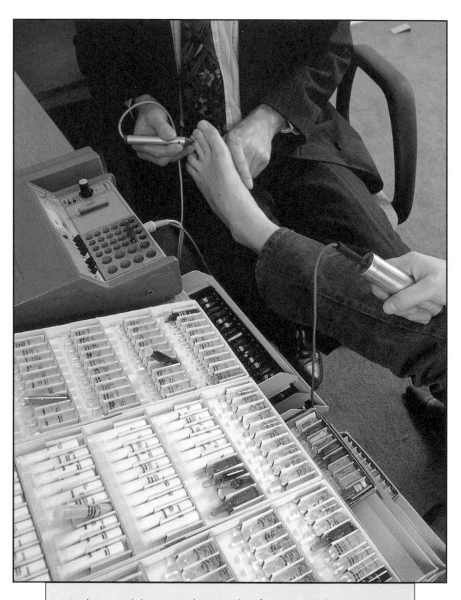

With possible remedies in the foreground, a practitioner of homeopathy performs a test on a patient to diagnose allergies.

eopathy also recommends the use of conventional treatment in cases of severe sickness.[24]

Advocates of homeopathy often point to research studies in major medical publications to support their contention that homeopathy is a valid treatment approach. But critics say that many clinical studies of homeopathy have been scientifically flawed. "Homeopathy's principles have been refuted by the basic sciences of chemistry, physics, pharmacology, and pathology. . . .," declares the National Council Against Health Fraud, a watchdog group. "Most homeopathic studies are of poor methodological quality, and are subject to bias. Homeopathic product labels do not provide sufficient information to judge their dosages. Although homeopathic remedies are generally thought to be nontoxic due to their high dilutions, some preparations have proved harmful."[25]

What's more, critics say that the Food and Drug Administration (FDA), which regulates homeopathic remedies, has not held them to the same standards as other drugs.

NATUROPATHY

Like homeopathy, naturopathy is an example of an alternative-medicine approach to treating illness. The National Institutes of Health describes it this way: "Naturopathy views disease as a manifestation of alterations in the processes by which the body naturally heals itself and emphasizes health restoration rather than disease treatment. Naturopathic physicians employ an array of healing practices, including diet and clinical nutrition; homeopathy; acupuncture; herbal medicine; hydrotherapy (the use of water in a range of temperatures and methods of application); spinal and soft-tissue manipulation; physical therapies involving

electric currents, ultrasound, and light therapy; therapeutic counseling; and pharmacology."[26]

AYURVEDA

Ayurveda means "science of life" and is the traditional
medical system of India, developed thousands of years
ago. Ayurveda puts an equal emphasis on mind, body,
and spirit, and seeks to maintain health by restoring
harmony and balance in a person. Ayurveda uses herbs,
massage, meditation, controlled breathing, and other
approaches. "At the heart of ayurveda is the concept
that all of existence comprises five basic principles or
elements: earth, air, fire, water, and ether. More than
their literal meaning, these terms represent principles of
action and interaction that guide and shape all that
exists on the material plane and in life processes," one
author says.

"The actions and interactions of these five elements
serve as the basis for understanding health, illness, individual constitution, and how to restore and maintain
harmony in the body."[27]

Chapter Three

THE MIND-BODY CONNECTION

Latisha's Story

Latisha was a bright youngster, but she had always had trouble concentrating in school. By the time she was in junior high, her grades in math, English, and science were suffering. Many days, her teachers would catch her staring out the classroom window or doodling aimlessly in her notebook.

Latisha knew she had a problem. When she was eight years old, her mother had taken her to a psychologist who diagnosed Latisha's difficulty as attention-deficit disorder, or ADD. The problem was distinguished from attention-deficit hyperactivity disorder (ADHD), which frequently involves the added symptom of hyperactivity, or an excess of nervous energy.

ADD is common among school-age children, and many adults struggle with it, too. Typically, those with the disorder find it extremely difficult to stay focused at school or work and to remember important assignments and responsibilities.

For several years Latisha took a drug called Ritalin for her attention disorder, but her problems in school persisted. Eventually, her mother became worried that taking the drug over a long period of time might have side effects for Latisha that would be worse than ADD itself. So Latisha and her mother decided to explore a different approach, called hypnotherapy, that uses no drugs at all. On the advice of a school counselor, they sought a consultation with Jack Reynolds, a professional hypnotist in their town.

Reynolds wondered whether Latisha did indeed have ADD. He noted that many youngsters who are told they have ADD are bright, normal kids who simply have trouble controlling their natural energy and curiosity. Not only that, he said, what looks like ADD could sometimes be a behaviorial problem caused by an allergy, a dietary deficiency, or a mineral imbalance in the child's system.

Reynolds felt that youngsters who do have ADD often can learn to manage their attention problems without drugs, using powers that have been within themselves all along. Hypnosis, he told Latisha and her mother, could unlock those powers in a safe way.

Latisha and her mother decided to give hypnosis a try. Reynolds spent part of the first appointment explaining hypnosis to Latisha and *her mother, establishing a rapport with Latisha, and talking with her about her physical and mental health, making sure that she was a suitable subject for hypnosis. Latisha then began her first session of hypnosis therapy.*

Reynolds asked Latisha to relax in a reclining chair as he spoke to her in a slow, soothing voice. Latisha was fully aware of her surroundings during the entire session, and Reynolds told her that she would neither say nor do anything during hypnosis that would violate the moral and ethical standards she set for herself in her everyday life, nor say anything that she would not want her mother to hear.

Still, by asking Latisha to imagine herself walking down a long country lane on a bright fall day, Reynolds was able to guide her to a state of deep concentration and relaxation. At that point, he began to make suggestions to Latisha that helped her see more clearly how she could better focus on her schoolwork. He also recommended some specific techniques for her to consider.

At the same time, he began to ask her about her fears and concerns about competing academically with her peers and how those fears might be causing Latisha to undermine her academic progress.

Latisha spoke of an older brother who had done well in high school and college and had gone on to medical school, where he was studying to be an orthopedic surgeon. She also spoke of her younger sister, who, at the age of seven, already was a budding performer in a local theater group.

It seemed, Latisha said, that she was concerned about measuring up to the success of her siblings. In making that discovery, Latisha could now begin to focus on her fears, concerns, strengths, and weaknesses. Meanwhile, her mother could give her the moral support she needed to succeed and to rebuild her self-esteem.

Latisha underwent five more sessions of hypnotherapy, and her performance at school improved considerably, even though she had stopped taking Ritalin. At times she still had trouble focusing and concentrating. But in the evenings, after a day when she caught herself daydreaming, she used a self-hypnosis technique that Reynolds taught her to help her refocus on school. After a while, Latisha was able to keep herself on track, and her grades improved.

More importantly, Latisha was able to recognize when she was unfairly comparing herself to her siblings. In time, she came to see herself as a unique person with talents and interests all her own.

Rikki's Story

When Rikki was eleven years old, he was brutally beaten and sexually assaulted by a man in his neighborhood, and as a result he stopped communicating with those around him. Internalizing his horrible experience, Rikki soon began displaying other signs of mental illness—depression, compulsive behavior, and aggression toward those who tried to get close to or communicate with him.

After a few months, Rikki was sent to live in a hospital for the mentally ill. There the doctors and counselors had no luck in their efforts to break through Rikki's wall of silence and anger, and for many months his prognosis seemed hopeless.

Then a caseworker noticed something important. One day Rikki was in his room, curled up on his bed in a fetal position, his face turned toward the wall, when suddenly the sounds of a Mozart concerto could be heard from a room down the hall. Rikki turned and lay on his back, opened his eyes, and began moving gently to the swells and strains of the music. When the music stopped abruptly—a nurse had closed the door of the room from which the sound came—Rikki again turned toward the wall, his body tight and motionless. The caseworker had a clue as to how to reach Rikki.

She consulted with Rikki's treatment team, which included a specialist trained in the field of music therapy, a discipline that uses music to achieve non-musical goals, such as to ease pain, soothe anxiety, treat people with physical or mental disabilities or addictive disorders, and comfort those who are terminally ill. The field of music therapy is not new—the Chinese have employed it for thousands of years, and ancient thinkers such as Aristotle, Plato, and Pythagoras recognized music's healing power.

In the West, music therapy is a health profession, the certified practitioners of which must meet national standards. The field gained popularity in the 1940s as soldiers who fought in World War II were treated with music for combat-related stress. In 1950 the National Association for Music Therapy was established, and today many universities offer formal programs of study in the discipline.

Even though some researchers say music therapy can have a direct effect on a person's physiological processes—heart rate and the release of pain-killing chemicals in the brain, for example—it remains unclear how music brings about those changes. What is clear, however, is that music can have great therapeutic value. The potential benefits include elevating a patient's mood, drawing him into interpersonal contact with those around him, creating an outlet for emotional expression, and providing a means of improving memory and physical dexterity.

In Rikki's case, the goal was to use music to try to draw him out of his emotional shell, to give him a means of self-expression, and to provide a safe way for him to release his pent-up anger and fear.

In sessions lasting an hour or so, sometimes with Rikki alone and sometimes in a room with other youngsters, the music therapist used a variety of treatment strategies. She first determined what kinds of music Rikki seemed most likely to respond to, and she confirmed what the counselor had noticed: He seemed to like classical music, and Mozart seemed to be his favorite composer of all.

The therapist began to see subtle changes in Rikki when he heard the music, and, using her own musical training and her interpersonal skills, she soon began to anticipate what tones and cadences might appeal to Rikki the most. One day she experienced a huge breakthrough in Rikki's therapy when he quietly asked her to replay a movement he had heard earlier in the session.

Eventually, Rikki came to choose some of the selections the therapist played, and the rapport between them grew to a point that Rikki could begin speaking about the emotions locked up inside him.

As she drew him out, the therapist gave Rikki some musical instruments to play himself—a drum at first, and later a small electronic keyboard. Rikki had never had musical training, but he beat the drum in regular and powerful beats, sometimes showing signs of anger as he swung the drumstick harder and harder. Often, Rikki would simply slide the stick over the skin of the drum in gentle movements, his eyes closing for long periods and his mouth set in a grimace.

One day, Rikki asked to bring the keyboard to a group meeting of emotionally disturbed youngsters, and, with much fanfare, he played a tune for the gathering, the first sign that he was reaching out to strangers around him.

As time progressed, Rikki became less repressed and more expressive. The music did not cure his emotional trauma, nor did it cover up the pain he felt. But it provided an avenue for him to begin to recover from his terrible experience and a way for him to relate to those around him.

Nathan's Story

Nathan was a hearty trucker, but one Monday morning just after sunup, he collapsed in the parking lot of a truck stop. His right arm was

47

paralyzed, his vision was blurred, and his speech was slurred. Luckily for Nathan, another trucker saw him collapse and called 911. A quick trip to the emergency room saved his life. After some tests, the doctors confirmed what Nathan already suspected: He'd had a mild stroke.

In a few days Nathan was able to speak clearly again, but he didn't regain use of his arm. Not only that, but his doctor told him that hypertension—high blood pressure—put him at great risk of another stroke. To help address both problems—his disabled arm and his high blood pressure—Nathan's doctor not only pre-scribed drugs, a low-salt diet, physical therapy, and other conventional approaches, but also suggested that he try a training program called biofeedback.

As modern as the approach sounded to Nathan, he soon learned that the principles of biofeedback are hundreds, if not thousands, of years old. In ancient China, shamans, or healers, could regulate various bodily functions such as heart rate, blood pressure, skin temper-ature, and other processes not normally thought to be under conscious control.

Experimentation on modern biofeedback began in the mid-twentieth century. In the early 1940s, researchers in the United States and Britain developed equipment to detect tiny physical responses in the body. By the late 1960s, American researchers had demonstrated that the method had therapeutic uses, and soon biofeedback clinics were springing up from coast to coast.

Nathan visited one of these clinics a few weeks after his stroke. There he learned about the basic theory of biofeedback and the tools the clinics would be using to help him.

First, the therapist told Nathan that a person could learn, through practice, deep relaxation, willpower, and other means to control such things as skin temperature, brain waves, the functioning of internal organs such as the bladder, and more.

For his hypertension, Nathan would be connected with electrodes to a computer that measured blood pressure, heart rate, and other metabolic functions, the therapist told him. The machine would enable Nathan to begin to keep track of his blood pressure and, through subtle physical, emotional, and mental adjustments, to regulate it.

Usually, people cannot tell when their blood pressure has changed, but a sensor attached to Nathan's skin would give him a clue of what was happening in his heart, arteries, and veins. The device would measure the temperature of his skin, providing a way to detect fluctuations in blood flow from changes in the expansion and contraction of his blood vessels. Another device—a finger pulse—might be used to measure Nathan's pulse rate and blood flow—and thus his heart activity, giving him clues as to whether he was anxious or nervous.

When Nathan's blood pressure dropped below a favorable target level, the biofeedback device would emit a tone, telling him he had succeeded, the therapist explained. That knowledge is a type of reward or encouragement for the patient. After consistent practice, Nathan was told, he could learn to help control his blood pressure with regularity. He even could learn to control stress—a factor in high blood pressure—by altering his brain waves, the therapist told him.

Nathan would use much the same approach to try to regain use of his disabled arm. In a process known as "electromyographic biofeedback," electrodes would be attached to his arm to monitor electrical impulses in the muscles. As Nathan tried to use the arm, the therapist told him, he would be able to tell how successful he was by watching the monitor. Over time, Nathan would learn to engage the muscle and influence its contractions and expansions, using the biofeedback monitor as a guide.

Nathan went to work on his arm and blood-pressure problems, displaying the same determination and energy he once showed in his days as a long-haul driver. He knew that the success of his biofeedback regimen would depend in large part on his willpower and attitude.

Nathan learned over several months to control his blood pressure, eventually keeping it close to 130 over 80. He also began to feel sensation in his crippled arm and, after learning how to engage the damaged muscle, began to regain limited use of the limb.

The work was not easy, especially that with the arm. There were many days when Nathan wanted to give up. But the health-care workers at the biofeedback clinic, along with his wife, doctor, and physical therapists, helped Nathan realize that physical factors once thought to be

beyond the influence of the mind could indeed
be consciously stimulated.

When people get sick, the first impulse is often to look for a physical cause—and a remedy that has physical attributes: the taste and smell of medicine, the keen cut of a scalpel, the firmness of a plaster cast.

But sometimes, illness and healing have an invisible quality, a mysterious aspect that defies conventional scientific understanding or direct observation.

Dr. Randolph Byrd, a cardiologist at the University of California at San Francisco Medical Center, made what some researchers believe is a remarkable discovery. Dr. Byrd found that prayer had a major impact on how 393 heart-attack victims in the hospital's cardiac-care unit fared. While all the patients received the same level of physical care, half were prayed for by name by prayer groups around the country. None of the patients, doctors, or nurses was aware of which patients received those prayers. But the group of patients who received prayers had fewer deaths, a faster recovery, and used fewer strong medications than the group that did not.[1]

No one knows exactly how prayer affects health, but a growing number of studies suggest that it does. That research is part of an even larger body of science indicating that the mind—though both conscious thought and unconscious brain activity—has a far-reaching effect on physical health.

"Mind and body are inextricably linked, and their second-by-second interaction exerts a profound influence upon health and illness, life and death," writes Kenneth R. Pelletier, a senior clinical fellow at Stanford University's Center for Research in Disease Prevention. "Attitudes, beliefs, and emotional states ranging from love and compassion to fear and anger can trigger chain reactions that affect blood chemistry, heart rate, and the activity of every cell and organ system in the body."

Uncertainties remain over the extent to which the mind can affect the body and how people can use the mind/body connection to prevent or overcome illness, Pelletier writes. Yet, he adds, "effective and responsible mind/body approaches are beginning to be used widely—in university and private clinics, in hospitals, and as an integral part of health promotion programs" at large corporations. In addition, he notes, groups such as the National Academy of Sciences and National Institutes of Health have investigated the mind/body connection.[2]

Emotions such as fear, hopelessness, optimism, and courage have a lot to do with whether a person can ward off illness or recover rapidly from it. However, unlike conventional medicine, which tends to focus on the visible and measurable aspects of health, mind-body medicine seeks to draw a link between physical healing and a person's thoughts, feelings, and beliefs.

Besides prayer, mind-body therapies include biofeedback, hypnosis, meditation, guided imagery, psychotherapy, and art and music therapy.

A major research breakthrough in mind-body medicine came in the 1970s, when Robert Ader, director of the Division of Behavioral and Psychosocial Medicine at the University of Rochester (New York) School of Medicine, working with immunologist Nicholas Cohen, discovered that the immune system can learn to respond to conditioning. Ader found that rats, whose illness-fighting powers are similar to those of humans, could be conditioned to suppress their immune systems in response to the sweet taste of saccharin.[3]

Ader played a key role in establishing the emerging field of psychoneuroimmunology (PNI), which examines the link between the immune system and the behavioral, nervous-system, and hormone functions of the body. The immune system, once thought to be autonomous, is actually subject to changes by the brain, PNI researchers have discovered. Scientists now believe that the mind is closely linked to many bodily functions, though they do not fully understand how.

The mind-body connection is beginning to be used on the clinical level in a way that antibiotics and X-ray machines, which are now common, were in decades past. At the Emmanuel Unit of St. Francis Hospital in Greenville, South Carolina, caregivers have used prayer and music therapy alongside conventional treatments to help patients.[4] At Duke University, a study of 4,000 North Carolina residents age 65 and older found that those who took part in religious activities were 40 percent less likely to suffer from high blood pressure.[5] And the Lutheran Theological Southern Seminary recently joined with the University of South Carolina School of Public Health in a national project, funded by the Carter Center in Atlanta, to find programs that bring together religious and medical people and to enhance training.[6]

The mind-body connection has major implications for alternative medicine. First, like many other aspects of alternative healing, mind-body therapy takes a holistic approach to health care, seeing the human being not as a series of separate systems but as a unified being.

In addition, if emotions can induce chemical changes in the body, as scientists widely believe, then new techniques may be found to treat cancer, heart disease, and other maladies—techniques that draw upon the power of the mind and emotions to fight disease and that do not involve surgery and other tools of conventional medicine.

Finally, in keeping with the overall philosophy of alternative therapy, mind-body medicine puts the patient, rather than the physician, at the center of the healing process. That does not mean that a patient can completely control every illness, and it certainly does not mean that an illness is simply "all in the patient's head." But a growing number of medical researchers believe that a patient's emotions and outlook often can have a significant effect on the course of an illness. The tools of conventional Western medicine, such as surgery and prescription drugs, may be just one aspect of the healing process. In many cases, patients may hold the key to how well they fare against an illness.

"If a patient's attitudes and perceptions and emotions make a difference in how the immune system functions, or in how the brain reacts to a given condition . . ., then the patient is at the center of medical treatment and care, and we have to talk about the patient as an active, vital participant in healing," says Dr. David Felten, professor of neurobiology and anatomy at the University of Rochester School of Medicine. "It doesn't come from the physician. It comes from the patient. The physician is just one other participant in the process of healing."[7]

Of course, mind-body medicine has limits and pitfalls, just as other medical approaches do. Relying on the mind to heal the body can give patients false hope and possibly persuade them to reject conventional therapies that could prolong their lives or cure a disease.

Some of the impulse to reject conventional medicine stems from religious convictions. A study published in *Pediatrics*, the journal of the American Academy of Pediatrics, found that four of every five sick children in the United States who died after their parents relied on faith healing probably could have lived if medical treatment had been sought.[8]

Often, however, it is the mental duress of illness that causes people to turn to unscrupulous or ill-trained healers who claim to have mind-body powers. "A lot of us in this field tend to be exceedingly conservative because of the charlatans and the snake-oil salesmen, who figure, What have they got to lose?" says Dr. Felten. "They prey on the desperate, and the elderly, and the dying, promising them all kinds of cures if only they follow their remedy, for the low, low price of whatever it turns out to be—all without any substantiation whatsoever."

Cancer patients are a prime target for scams that try to get people to reject traditional Western medicine in favor of unproven alternative therapies. "It's a cruel hoax to try to pull people away from traditional medicine into totally unfounded and unsubstantiated approaches to cancer," Dr. Felten says. "Usually, what you find is that the people who are practicing this kind of approach are lashing out at medicine, claiming that medicine has totally failed in the treatment of cancer, which, of course, is ridiculous."[9]

Another pitfall of mind-body medicine is that patients will come to believe that their body is under their complete mental control and that illness is merely a sign of some sort of mental weakness. It is important to remember that scientists have much to learn yet about the connection between consciousness and illness, and no responsible practitioner would jump to the conclusion that a physical affliction always has a mental cause. In a letter to the *New England Journal of Medicine* in 1979, psychologists Dean H. Shapiro and Johanna Shapiro cautioned against the "distortion" in thinking that encourages people to reject conventional medical treatment in favor of novel, unproven theories about the power of the mind to heal physical illness. "This distortion maintains that the powers of self-control and of the

55

human mind are literally limitless in their capacity to influence the course of illness," they wrote.[10]

Still, the link between mind and body has encouraged the use of many techniques that advocates say can have therapeutic benefits. Here are a few of the most common mind-body approaches and how they are sometimes applied.

Guided Imagery

A person practicing guided imagery uses his or her imagination to create what might be called an "internal reality"—a series of thoughts, ideas, imaginary sights, sounds, and smells and other sensations that have an effect on the central nervous system.

Guided imagery is frequently used in the medical setting to control chronic pain. It also may be used to help control blood pressure, boost the immune system in AIDS patients, treat intestinal disorders, and address other health problems.

In using guided imagery, a patient may focus on a predetermined mental picture chosen to help control a specific symptom or gain an understanding of a personal problem. For example, someone suffering chronic back pain may conjure up a pleasing image of a flower-filled valley, concentrating on the sights, smells, and other sensations of the scene. By thinking about the valley, the patient's attention may be diverted away from the unpleasantness of the pain.

Advocates of guided imagery say it is more than a diversionary strategy, however. Some research studies suggest that imagery may have physiological benefits such as lower blood pressure, a decrease in pain, and enhanced immune-system response.

In addition, guided imagery can help a patient gain valuable insight into the psychological dimensions of a physical problem. Dr. Martin L. Rossman, codirector of the Academy for Guided Imagery in Mill Valley, California, told of a 24-year-old man with asthma who discovered through the use of imagery that he had unconsciously used his illness for emotional reasons, including coping with difficulties related to romantic closeness. Dr. Rossman encouraged the young man to communicate with a character in the image to overcome the problem and to imagine a means by which he could allow some individuals in his life to pass "checkpoints" along the "'roads' to his heart."[11]

Hypnosis

Like guided imagery, hypnosis is a form of highly focused concentration. It is commonly used to help people control addictions, cope with behavioral problems such as attention-deficit disorder, increase the ability to concentrate on schoolwork or other tasks, undergo dental procedures, sleep better, and deal with chronic pain.

Sometimes hypnosis is used alongside conventional medical treatment. Instead of relying on a chemical anesthetic for a tooth extraction, for example, a patient may be able to block out the pain of the procedure under the guidance of a hypnotist.

Hypnotism works by making a person highly open to suggestion. However, no one can be hypnotized against his or her wishes.

The aim of hypnosis is to put the conscious mind at rest and activate the unconscious mind. A typical treatment session begins with a request that the subject relax. Then, at the suggestion of the hypnotist (or the subject himself, in self-hypnosis), attention is shifted away from the immediate surroundings to a specific object or idea.

Hypnosis involves activating the unconscious mind to make it more receptive to a desired change.

During hypnosis, the subject is not asleep. In fact, the hypnotized individual is quite aware of his or her surroundings. Not only that, experts in hynosis say, the person will not do something that goes against his or her moral or ethical beliefs. And the individual may simply choose not to respond to a suggestion from the hypnotist.

While anyone has the potential to be hypnotized, the degree to which a person can be hynotized varies with the individual.

If you use a hypnotist, be sure the person has undergone thorough training and has the approval of an organization such as the National Guild of Hypnotists or the American Society of Clinical Hypnosis.

Biofeedback

Biofeedback is a method of learned control of biological functions, including body temperature, heart rate, blood pressure, muscle contraction, and brain waves.

Among the pioneers of biofeedback research were Elmer and Alyce Green, of the Menninger Foundation in Topeka, Kansas. In the early 1960s, the pair were taking a woman's skin temperature to chart her physiological changes during relaxation exercises. The Greens noticed that the woman's hand temperature suddenly rose 10 degrees. The woman told them that a migraine headache she'd been feeling went away at that same moment. The Greens then developed a biofeedback temperature device and taught people how to ease migraine headaches by using relaxation exercises to raise their hand temperatures.[12] The link between hand temperature and headache pain pointed to an important aspect of biofeedback theory: If a person could learn to control a biological function such as body temperature, pain and other disorders might be controlled.

Biofeedback is used today to treat a wide variety of illnesses and emotional and behavior problems, including heartbeat irregularities, migraine headaches, stress, and asthma. Often, biofeedback is used to promote relaxation, enhancing the effectiveness of other therapies or helping to ward off illness or stress.

Meditation

Unlike biofeedback, which requires technology for administering it, meditation is a solitary, contemplative discipline that can be learned in any setting. It is practiced in many religions, including Buddhism, Hinduism, Christianity, and Islam, but it does not require belief in a creed or philosophy. In the West, meditation in secular settings is an increasingly popular method to control stress.

One can think of meditation as a mental or spiritual state of peace and heightened awareness brought about by the contemplation of an object, idea, image, repeated phrase—or mantra—or even the absence of thought. It can have a variety of physical and emotional benefits, including reduction in muscle tension and heart rate and a change in brain-wave patterns that signals a state of deep relaxation.

Dr. Herbert Benson, founding president of the Mind/Body Medical Institute of New England Deaconess Hospital and the Harvard University Medical School, played a key role in identifying a phenomenon he calls the "relaxation response," a state of relaxation brought about by a form of Eastern transcendental meditation. By eliminating mental distraction and silently repeating a word, phrase, or short prayer upon exhalation for 10 to 20 minutes a day with eyes closed and muscles relaxed, a person can induce a variety of favorable physiological changes, Benson found. Those responses include a drop in breathing rates and oxygen intake, and a shift in brain waves toward a slower, relaxed state.

"The relaxation response can help in the treatment of many medical problems; in some cases, it can eliminate them entirely," according to Benson. "It's important to remember that most diseases have many different possible causes and contributing factors, and the relaxation response targets only one: stress. But this is no small feat, because stress alone can precipitate a wide range of unhealthy conditions. . . ."[13]

While the mind can be an important healing tool, so too can the sense of touch. In the next chapter, you will learn about a variety of touch therapies, some of which draw on the mind-body connection.

Chapter Four

TOUCH THERAPY: HANDS THAT SEEK TO HEAL

Jason's Story

After Jason was nearly killed in a motorcycle accident, he faced a long series of surgeries to repair fractures in his spine, pelvis, shoulder, and thigh. Three such operations had already taught Jason that he did not tolerate surgical anesthesia well. After each operation, he vomited for several days, and his doctors had to put him on powerful and debilitating painkillers to ease the misery of the recovery.

Facing the scalpel again—this time to fuse two vertebrae in his lower spine—Jason asked his doctor if it would make sense to try acupuncture as a way of relieving the post-operative nausea and pain he had experienced before.

While in the hospital, Jason had heard on TV that a panel convened by the National Institutes of Health had endorsed acupuncture as an effective treatment for some kinds of nausea, including nausea associated with surgical anesthesia. The panel also said that acupuncture could be effective in combating pain from dental surgery.

Jason's doctor was not very familiar with acupuncture, and at first he was skeptical. But after reading about the history of the procedure and reviewing the NIH panel's conclusions, he told Jason that acupuncture was worth a try.

A physician in town, Dr. Chen, was a licensed acupuncturist, one of 4,000 U.S. medical doctors to have that designation and one of 10,000 licensed acupuncturists nationwide.[1] Jason and his doctor consulted with Dr. Chen, who described to them both the ancient Chinese belief about acupuncture and the Western medical interpretation of the procedure.

Dr. Chen talked about the opposing but complementary forces of yin and yang. When these forces become unbalanced, the flow of vital energy, or chi, *along fourteen major channels, or meridians, is disrupted, he said. Disruption of* chi *along any of the meridians can cause pain or illness. By inserting fine needles into the skin or performing other procedures along the meridians, an acupuncturist can restore the proper flow of* chi, *he said.*

Dr. Chen also explained some of the modern theories about acupuncture. Those theories include the notions that electrical or neurochemical currents flow inside the body, and that acupuncture may release chemicals or stimulate the brain in a way that relieves pain and nausea.

With little to lose, Jason decided to ask Dr. Chen to perform acupuncture on him after his next operation. Dr. Chen thoroughly reviewed Jason's medical history. After the surgery, Dr. Chen inserted about a dozen needles, each as slender and fine as a human hair, into special points in Jason's skin, twirling the needles gently. He left them in for a half hour or so and then removed them swiftly, leaving few traces.

When Jason was fully awake, he was pleased that he felt no sensation of nausea from the anesthesia. During the next several days, Jason underwent several more acupuncture treatments to relieve pain from the surgery. He felt only a slight sensation from the needles being inserted.

"I've never been through an operation with so little nausea and pain," he told his regular physician and Dr. Chen. "I'm not sure how acupuncture works, but it seems to have helped me."

Simon's Story

Simon had studied the violin since he was six years old, and by the time he was 10 he was performing with adults in a local symphony. At 15 Simon won a national violin competition, and at 24 he was concertmaster of a metropolitan symphony orchestra.

But when he was 33, all of Simon's success came crashing down. A vague feeling of discomfort in his right wrist grew quickly into sharp, debilitating pain along his entire forearm, accompanied by muscular weakness in his hand.

The affliction made it difficult for him to hold his bow, let alone glide it masterfully over the strings of his instrument as he had done for many years.

Simon's doctor diagnosed him with carpal tunnel syndrome, a compression of nerves in the wrist that causes pain, numbness, and weakness. The physician prescribed a regimen of rest, special exercises, anti-inflammatory drugs, and painkillers. Simon felt little relief from the treatment, however, and the drugs had side effects, including drowsiness.

After a few months Simon's doctor suggested that surgery might be an option. Simon was desperate to revive his flagging musical career but leery of an operation that might cause him permanently to lose control in his right hand. He decided to investigate alternative treatments that would not be so invasive.

After informing his doctor of his intent and learning how to avoid using a harmful mix of alternative and conventional therapies, Simon went to work. First, he visited a specialist in acupressure, a treatment similar to acupuncture but carried out without needles.

The acupressure specialist taught Simon how to apply pressure to a point near his right wrist and told him to repeat the exercise at home three times a day. Simon also learned about other acupressure treatments, including ones thought to relieve stress and insomnia—problems that he was struggling with because of the disruption in his music career.

In addition, Simon consulted a nutritionist, who said that dietary changes could help him heal. For example, sugar, caffeine, and processed grains can cause a deficiency in vitamin B$_6$, she told Simon, a shortage that often is found in people who suffer from carpal tunnel syndrome. She recommended that Simon increase his intake of foods rich in vitamin B$_6$, including whole grains and fish. Simon resisted her suggestion that he take vitamin supplements, fearing that they would build up to harmful levels in his body. Finally, Simon tried using a mixture of anti-inflammatory herbs.

The alternative treatments didn't work. While the pain in Simon's wrist decreased for a while, that may have been because he played the violin only occasionally as he tried to heal. Once he began practicing in earnest again, the numbness, pain, and loss of control returned.

Eventually, Simon underwent surgery for his problem, and a year later he was back with his beloved symphony. It was Western medicine, and not alternative therapy, that had restored his wrist to usefulness. Even so, Simon continued to follow some of the dietary and acupressure measures he learned, and he believed they helped him remain healthy long after his carpal-tunnel problem was cured.

Irene's Story

At 84 years of age, Irene still did The New York Times crossword puzzle every day and read two books a week, everything from Agatha Christie mysteries to nonfiction works on science and history. Yet as mentally alert as Irene was, she was worn down by physical conditions common to old age. She suffered from high blood pres-

sure, aching and stiff joints, and chronic fatigue. Once an avid orchid grower, she had given up gardening because of her physical problems. The small patch of earth outside her bedroom window lay untended and weed-choked.

One day, looking through a book on Chinese medicine, Irene found a chapter on qigong—pronounced "chee gong"—denoting energy cultivation or enrichment.

A tradition that is thousands of years old, medical qigong combines physical and breathing exercises with meditation. By integrating the mind, body, and spirit, qigong seeks to build up a person's vital energy—chi—and direct it to strategic points of the body, facilitating healing and wellness.

Irene read that tens of millions of people in China practice qigong, and that it is appropriate for people of all ages. Not only that, it could be a very useful therapy for the kinds of problems, such as high blood pressure and arthritis, that afflicted her. And while it could take a lifetime to become a master of one of the many types of qigong, the average person could learn some basic techniques in a just a few months. Irene decided to try.

In her local newspaper, Irene learned of a qigong group, supervised by a knowledgeable practitioner, that was set to begin classes at the city's community center. When Irene arrived the following week, she joined a group of 20 people—one as young as 15, another 78—who said they'd come to try to overcome an existing health problem or to learn to take better care of themselves and ward off illness and stress.

The instructor told the group that qigong *is more than exercise. It's a way of training one's breathing and thinking to maximize the circulation of* chi *in the body. It is not a panacea, he continued. For* qigong *to work, the student must practice it diligently, show a positive attitude, and hone a sense of willpower and concentration.*

As Irene's qigong *classes began, she heard many terms that were unfamiliar to her. Indeed, the vocabulary of* qigong, *like much of the terminology of Asian medicine, is foreign to most people in the West. Not only does* chi, *or energy, flow along fourteen invisible pathways of the body, affecting a person's balance of* yin *and* yang, *it flows along finer channels and networks covering every bit of tissue.*

Irene was skeptical when she read about such claims because they have not been proven using the rigorous scientific standards of Western medicine. Still, from her very first class, Irene could see benefits to qigong, *especially its emphasis on breathing, movement, mental focusing, and relaxation.*

As her qigong *instructor explained, the technique can help reduce blood pressure, enhance the delivery of oxygen to the body's cells and tissues, boost the immune system, improve the capabilities of the endocrine system, and help with blood circulation, among other things.*

Irene began slowly with just a few simple qigong *exercises. One exercise, which was designed to aid the heart and digestive functions, involved slowly raising the arms to the side of the body, turning the hands in a certain way, then lowering the arms while doing a breathing exercise.*

She also learned to use a set of colorful qigong *therapy balls, round objects that emit musical tones when they are rotated among the fingers. The exercise is said to strengthen the tendons in the hand and massage the hand's acupuncture points, helping with blood circulation, muscle tone, and mental health.*

Irene did not try to do exercises she did not feel physically prepared for, and she enjoyed her classes. Soon, she was able to practice qigong *on her own. She felt invigorated by the exercises, and she experienced improvements in her blood pressure level and joint problems. When spring came, she began planting flowers again.*

Rex's Story

Rex, a 7-year-old Akita, had always been a graceful dog, romping happily around the 12-acre farm where he lived and effortlessly keeping his owner's livestock in line. But as Rex got older, he showed signs of discomfort in his hindquarters, and one summer day he began to limp as he made his way through the pasture.

Tim, Rex's owner, asked his veterinarian to check out the dog's problem. After X rays and other tests, he gave the diagnosis: Rex suffered from canine hip dysplasia, a degenerative disease of the hip joint that is passed on genetically. While the disease cannot be cured, the veterinarian told Tim that there was a good chance it could be managed in a way that Rex could continue to lead a fairly normal and active life.

But that, the vet continued, would depend on what course of treatment Tim chose for Rex.

As with many diseases afflicting pets and humans, a variety of potential treatments existed. Surgery was one. But as the veterinarian explained to Tim, surgery was not a great choice because of the cost and risks involved. Drugs also posed problems because of their potential side effects, including suppression of the immune system and internal bleeding.

Unhappy with these options, Tim asked his veterinarian what other recourse there might be for Rex. To his surprise, the veterinarian suggested a variety of holistic therapies—the same approach Tim knew as "alternative medicine" for humans. Acupuncture, chiropractic, and vitamin therapy were sometimes effective in managing the symptoms of canine hip dysplasia, the veterinarian told Tim.

In fact, the vet continued, alternative-medicine techniques, including homeopathy, were being used by more and more veterinarians. In 1996, in fact, the American Veterinary Medical Association, with more than 61,000 U.S. and Canadian members, issued guidelines for alternative-medicine practice on animals, although the guidelines did not signify an endorsement of such procedures.[2]

Of course, like many alternative-medicine therapies used to treat humans, much remains unknown about how the treatments work and how effective they are. Rigorous clinical trials, peer review, and scholarly documentation are still lacking for many treatment regimens, the veterinarian explained. And concepts such as chi, *or vital energy, that are central to acupuncture and other forms of Asian medicine seem beyond reason or proof at this point, he said.*

Still, the vet said, he had heard enough stories of animals treated successfully with alterna-

tive approaches to believe that they are worth trying, especially when conventional treatments posed problems. Tim agreed.

The next day, he took Rex to a veterinary specialist in alternative medicine. After evaluating the dog and reviewing the other veterinarian's diagnosis, she and Tim settled on a four-part course of treatment for Rex: chiropractic, acupuncture, nutritional therapy, and physical therapy.

She first treated Rex with a type of spinal adjustment designed to realign vertebrae in the dog's spine. Misalignment could have been causing symptoms similar to those of hip dysplasia. The treatment, she said, would aid in clearing the neurological channels in Rex's hindquarters and help the tissues in his hip function better.

The specialist also began a series of acupuncture treatments on Rex, inserting extremely fine needles into strategic points of the tissue. The Chinese believe the procedure rebalances the flow of chi in the body, she told Tim, but no one really knows how acupuncture works. She said she believed the procedure somehow stimulated electric impulses in the tissue and blocked pain to the affected region.

The specialist also prescribed a nutritional supplement for Rex to reduce the inflammation in his hip joint. She suggested several different vitamins, explaining that she was being careful in choosing the exact form and dosage to reduce the chances of side effects.

Finally, the specialist asked Tim to do physical-therapy exercises with Rex, guiding the *joint gently through a series of movements. By doing this several times a day, Tim could help Rex regenerate his muscle in the affected area and keep the dog from developing new problems with the cartilage and other tissue in his hip.*

Tim followed the specialist's advice, and Rex got better, although he never again ran through the pasture with the same ease that he displayed as a puppy. From time to time his hip problem flared up, and Tim returned him to the specialist for treatment. Rex lived to an old age, free of surgery or debilitating drugs.

As these stories illustrate, the body has many mysterious ways of freeing itself from sickness and pain. Touch and movement are ways of bringing about such healing.

A gentle caress, deep massage, stimulation of the body with acupuncture needles, the ancient Chinese practice of *qigong*, or some other kind of contact or movement can have important physical and psychological benefits. Alternative medicine includes a variety of therapies that use touch and other forms of physical stimulation. Some of them have gained wide acceptance in mainstream medicine. Other therapies, including ones in which practitioners claim to be able to sense a patient's "energy field," remain highly controversial.

One of the most basic touch therapies is therapeutic massage, a systematic manipulation of the soft tissues by a trained practitioner. Massage can have a variety of benefits, including helping to increase blood flow in the muscles, relieve localized pain and discomfort, and create a sense of well-being. Even so, massage is not advisable for undiagnosed medical conditions. Nor is it good for certain health problems, such as open wounds and tumors.

CHIROPRACTIC

Besides massage, another prevalent form of touch-related therapy is chiropractic, which involves the manipulation of the spine and other parts of the body to alleviate pain and restore proper nerve function. This therapeutic approach has been around for thousands of years in its basic form. The ancient Greeks, for example, practiced spinal manipulation. But modern chiropractic has existed for only about a hundred years.

In the late 1800s, Daniel David Palmer, an Iowa grocer who was interested in the workings of the human body, theorized that adjustment of the spine could be employed to maintain good health. He had examined a man who had been deaf for 17 years after injuring his spine. Palmer discovered that a vertebra was out of alignment at the point of injury. After Palmer adjusted the vertebra, the man could hear again.

Advocates of chiropractic believe that the body becomes susceptible to disease when there is interference with the healthy functioning of tissue. Such interference, they believe, is caused by subluxation, or the misalignment of the spinal vertebrae, which interferes with nerve impulses and prevents the body from properly regulating the tissues connected to those neural pathways.

For decades, chiropractic was viewed as little more than quackery by the American medical establishment. But in 1980 the American Medical Association recognized this branch of medicine. A study by the U.S. Department of Health and Human Services in 1994 concluded that spinal manipulation is effective in

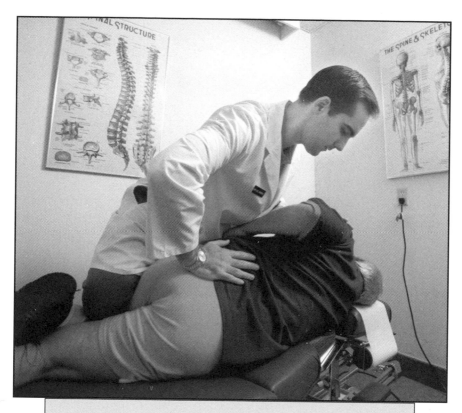

A chiropractor works on a patient to adjust his spine and help restore balance and health to the patient's body.

relieving acute lower-back pain and that it works better than surgery, drug therapy, and other conventional treatments.[3]

Chiropractic is growing rapidly in the United States. By the year 2010 it is projected that more than 100,000 chiropractors will be working in the United States.[4] Some insurance companies have even been persuaded to cover chiropractic treatments. Even so, many critics argue that more research is needed into the healing powers and potential physical risks of chiropractic.

A recent outgrowth of chiropractic is a therapy known as applied kinesiology, which looks for imbalances in the organs and glands by evaluating muscle strength.

Other touch treatments include:

- **Rolfing**—works to achieve the proper alignment of the head, torso, legs, and other parts of the body.
- **Reflexology**—a therapy in which pressure is applied to precise areas of the body, especially the feet, to relieve stress, improve blood supply to organs, glands, and other body parts, help to unblock nerve pathways, and restore balance in the body.

ACUPUNCTURE

Acupuncture has gained a new measure of acceptance among medical researchers in the West. The procedure was largely unknown in the West until the early 1970s, when the journalist James Reston underwent emergency surgery in China with nothing but acupuncture to kill the postoperative pain. Reston wrote about his experience, igniting interest in the procedure. Since then, acupuncture has become one of the most widely embraced alternative treatments, with as many as 15 million Americans having tried the procedure at least once, according to some estimates.[5]

In 1997, a 12-member panel of medical experts convened by the National Institutes of Health declared that acupuncture is an effective treatment for relieving nausea associated with pregnancy, surgical anesthesia, and chemotherapy, and pain from dental surgery. The panel also found less clear evidence that acupuncture could be useful in treating muscle and skeletal problems such as fibromyalgia and tennis elbow.[6]

"There is sufficient evidence of acupuncture's value to expand its use into conventional medicine and to encourage further studies of its physiology and clinical value," said the panel, which was headed by Dr. David J. Ramsay, a physiologist.[7]

The panel's conclusions about acupuncture were controversial. "What the proponents present as evidence is in fact delusion," says Victor Herbert, a professor of medicine at Mount Sinai School of Medicine in New York City. Dr. Herbert, who went to China to investigate acupuncture, concluded that for the most part it was a matter of hypnotic suggestion.[8]

Still, many medical specialists offer at least a limited defense of acupuncture. "It's a very difficult task to take a completely different system of medicine, transplant it to a system of Western medicine, and ask, 'Does it work?'" Dr. Ramsay said. "But we did decide that in a number of situations, it really does work."[9]

How acupuncture works isn't entirely clear. According to traditional Chinese medical theory, when thin needles are inserted into selective points on the surface of the body, they affect the flow of energy along a series of invisible meridians deep in the tissue and bring it into equilibrium. The meridians relate to organs such as the heart, liver, lungs, and kidneys, and acupuncture restores equilibrium to the organs and promotes health.

In the West, researchers tend to doubt theories about meridians and invisible energy flow. Some speculate that acupuncture works by releasing such substances as endorphins, which are neurochemicals that can reduce pain and affect the body in other ways. Other researchers believe that acupuncture subtly affects nerve pathways in the body, inhibiting sensa-

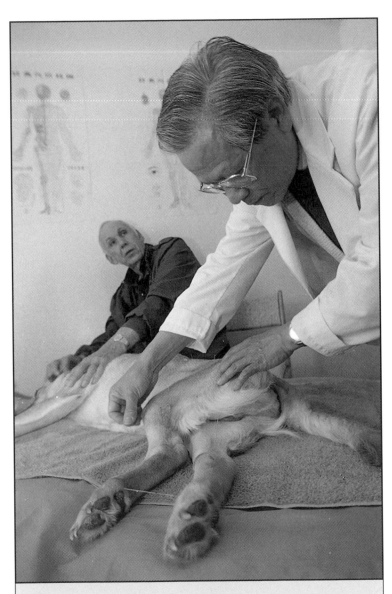

As noted in Rex's story, acupuncture and other alternative therapies are sometimes used even on animals.

tions of pain. Relatively few Western physicians view acupuncture as a viable replacement for surgical anesthetic. Still, clinical studies suggest that acupuncture does indeed work in specific circumstances.

In a study published in the *Journal of the Royal Society of Medicine* in 1988, Professor John Dundee of Queen's University in Belfast, Ireland, found that when a point near the creases of the wrist was stimulated with an acupuncture needle, the nausea and vomiting associated with early pregnancy was relieved or eliminated.[10]

A later study in the *British Journal of Anaesthesia* said that the same wrist acupoint could be used to treat nausea associated with general anesthesia and chemotherapy.[11]

In a dental study, people who used acupuncture before the removal of impacted molars endured an average of only 17 minutes of postoperation pain, compared with 94 minutes among those treated with conventional drugs.[12]

While much is still unknown about acupuncture, the NIH panel said that it is safe and relatively free of side effects when done properly. And however it may work, acupuncture's promises as a therapeutic tool are compelling.

ACUPRESSURE

Like acupuncture, acupressure is based on the ancient Asian concept of *chi*, or vital energy. Using fingers or thumbs, the practitioner applies strong pressure at key points to induce healing and relieve pain. Asian medical experts believe these points of the body fall along invisible meridians, or energy channels. Through pressure exerted downward or in line with the channel's energy flow, they believe, acupressure rebalances a person's vital energy and allows it to flow freely, restoring health to the distressed region of the body.

Many western researchers doubt the existence of *chi*, however. They tend to see acupressure as a form of deep massage that stimulates blood flow to an affected area and perhaps generates electrical impulses or releases chemicals that block pain and aid healing. Still, they have not ruled out acupressure's potential benefits. Clinical studies have supported the usefulness of some strategic acupressure points, and acupressure therapy is gaining popularity in the United States and other Western nations.

QIGONG

Used for fitness and healing, *qigong* has elements of meditation, movement, relaxation techniques, and breathing exercises. *Qigong* requires daily practice. The goal is to build up the body's flow of *chi* and direct it to appropriate spots to enhance health and promote healing.

A controversial aspect of *qigong* is known as "external healing." Some advocates claim that *qigong* masters can actually direct their vital energy toward another person, healing them through mysterious powers that seem to defy logic and human experience. One study, by Fong Li-da, M.D., of the Beijing Institute of Traditional Chinese Medicine, concluded that a *qigong* master could project her *chi* to either kill bacteria or promote its growth in test tubes.[13]

THERAPEUTIC TOUCH

Perhaps no alternative technique has been so widely embraced and, at the same time, so broadly criticized, as therapeutic touch.

The approach, a modern form of such ancient healing practices as the laying on of hands, was developed in the early 1970s by Dr. Dolores Krieger, a nursing professor at New York University, and Dora Kunz, a healer. Advocates of therapeutic touch believe the human body has energy fields that a trained practitioner can feel. A therapist seeks to detect and correct any disruptions in these energy fields.

"Disease is seen as a condition of energy imbalance or blocked energy flow. Assessment is done by passing the hands over the body from head to toe at about two to four inches above the surface. The practitioner then serves as a conduit for universal energy, consciously and actively transferring energy into the recipient. The hands are used to direct and focus the energy, sometimes in rhythmical, sweeping motions."[14]

The feel of a human energy field has been described in such ways as cold, hot, tingling, throbbing, and "tactile as taffy."[15] Dr. Krieger described the feel of the energy field as a sensation of "warm Jell-O or warm foam."[16]

Therapeutic touch is taught to nursing students around the world, and Dr. Krieger said she has trained more than 47,000 practitioners.[17] Advocates claim that therapeutic touch can relieve pain, ease stress, treat some diseases, and soothe crying babies.

Yet some in the medical establishment have always viewed therapeutic touch with deep suspicion. A research study published in *The Journal of the American Medical Association* in 1998 challenged the claims of Dr. Krieger and her supporters.[18]

The study was designed and conducted by a grade-school student named Emily Rosa of Loveland, Colorado. The research report on the study was prepared by Emily's mother, Linda, a nurse and critic of touch therapy; Larry Sarner of the National

Those who practice *qigong* tout its healing properties and its many other benefits to the body.

Therapeutic Touch Study Group, which questions the approach; and Dr. Stephen Barrett of Quackwatch, a non-profit group that posts information on the Internet about controversial medical practices. Emily tested the claims of therapeutic touch in a fourth-grade science-fair experiment.[19]

Twenty-one therapeutic-touch practitioners took part in the experiment. They had experience in the technique ranging from one to 27 years. Emily tested them to find out whether they could determine which of their hands was closest to her own hand by sensing its energy field. Emily placed her hand over either the right or left hand of a practitioner, letting it hover there. Placement of her hand was decided by flipping a coin. A tall screen prevented the practitioners from seeing where Emily was placing her hand.

The practitioners identified the correct hand in only 44 percent of 280 trials—close to the rate that would be expected by random chance. To prove touch therapy's validity, the study's authors maintained, "the practitioners should have been able to locate the investigator's hand 100 percent of the time. . . . Their failure to substantiate [therapeutic touch's] most fundamental claim is unrefuted evidence that the claims of [therapeutic touch] are groundless and that further professional use is unjustified," the study concluded.[20]

In a news report of the study, advocates of therapeutic touch defended the practice and said the experiment lacked validity. "It works," Dr. Krieger said of the technique. She went on to say that Emily Rosa "completely misunderstood what the nature of basic research is."[21]

But in a note appended to the study, Dr. George D. Lundberg, the editor of the journal, called the experiment a "simple, statistically valid study" that "tests the theoretical basis for 'Therapeutic Touch': 'the human energy field.' This study found that such a field does not exist." Lundberg added that practitioners of therapeutic touch "should disclose these [study] results to patients . . . and patients should save their money and refuse to pay for this procedure until or unless additional honest experimentation demonstrates an actual effect."[22]

Lundberg's note also included a useful caveat about the entire field of unconventional therapy. "The

American public is fascinated by alternative . . . medicine," he wrote. "Some of these practices have a valid scientific basis; some of them are proven hogwash; many of them have never been adequately tested scientifically." Therapeutic touch, Lundberg added, "falls into the latter classification."[23]

Chapter Five

LOOKING INTO THE FUTURE

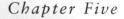

A newspaper ad from a prominent department store in the Washington, D.C., area promoted one of the latest innovations in alternative medicine: a "magnetic-wave" device for the sale price of $49.99. The device, the ad claimed, "relieves pain, improves blood flow and [the] body's natural healing process. Apply magnets to virtually any body area."

Some clinical research indeed suggests that magnets may aid in treating pain, broken bones, and depression. But magnetic therapy is in its infancy. Many practitioners of conventional medicine consider it of no medical value.

Research on magnetic therapy remains under way. But whether magnets are effective treatment tools or not, the ad is a telling sign of how much alternative medicine is becoming part of the American culture. As consumer interest in unconventional health care continues to mushroom, the demand will help to shape the course of medicine: its cost, availability, style, regulation, and variety of treatment options.

One of the most important factors in the future expansion of alternative medicine is whether private health-insurance companies will agree to cover alternative therapies.

"This [alternative medicine] business is burgeoning, but its biggest challenge is going to be integrating it with traditional medicine and with insurance coverage," says Dr. Richard Sheff, the president of CommonWell, Inc. This Massachusetts company develops certification programs for alternative therapists to meet the concerns of insurance companies.[1]

Even though many insurers refrain from covering alternative therapies, the scene is changing as health-insurance companies seek to satisfy consumer demand and to overcome concerns that insurers aren't doing enough to serve the needs of the public.

In a recent survey of 114 senior HMO executives by Landmark Healthcare Inc., a health-care company that focuses on alternative medicine, 85 percent said they thought that the relationship between traditional and alternative medicine will grow closer. Nearly three-fourths of HMOs believe that consumer demand for alternative care will be moderate or strong in the future, the survey found.[2]

"Even with skeptics and some research refuting successful treatment findings, consumer demand has forced health care companies to at least consider incorporating [complementary and alternative medical insurance] benefits," *Risk Management*, a publication that covers insurance issues, noted recently. "As its popularity has spread from the West Coast to the East, health plan providers are realizing the advantage of offering additional choice to distinguish themselves in an often maligned industry."[3]

As *Risk Management* noted, the growth of insurance coverage for some alternative therapies largely grew out of trends that began on the West Coast. Labor shortages in the high technology field have helped prompt employers to expand medical benefits to attract workers. Many workers argue that alternative therapies are more cost effective and less harsh than surgery or synthetic drugs.

In 1996, the state of Washington mandated that insurance companies and medical plans cover health-care expenses for all licensed, certified, or registered practitioners, including massage therapists, naturopaths, and acupuncturists.[4] Enactment of the law signaled that consumers and alternative-medicine practitioners were having some success at forcing the medical and insurance establishment to face the rise of unconventional medicine. Workers covered by company-sponsored health insurance are pushing their employers to include acupuncture, chiropractic, and other therapies in the list of covered treatment options.

Yet rising consumer demand has created a dilemma for insurance companies and health-care providers. In an era when doctors, hospitals, health-maintenance organizations, and insurance companies are under pressure to provide the highest quality care at the lowest cost, few insurance companies want to spend money on unproven therapies that may or may not help patients. In many cases, quality research on alternative medicine has not caught up with public demand for the therapies.

Such research takes big sums of money and months or years to accomplish. Some of those studies are being done by universities and government, as noted earlier in this book. But because much medical research is funded by pharmaceutical companies—and because much alternative medicine shuns prescription drugs in favor of natural remedies—there is little incentive for drug manufacturers to pay for clinical trials in alternative medicine. A lack of research funds could impede the gathering of convincing data to prove or disprove the claims of alternative-medicine advocates.

Even with inconclusive or questionable research, however, consumers are finding ways to obtain health insurance that covers alternative therapy. For example, some insurance companies have sold what is known in the industry as a "rider." That is a plan sold to people at a slightly higher cost than regular medical insurance to provide extra coverage. By offering riders, insurance companies are saying, in effect, that if people are willing to pay extra for insurance to cover alternative therapies, the companies will make the coverage available.

As reimbursement options grow, it is likely that alternative medicine will have more visibility and legitimacy in the eyes of the public, business officials, and government regulators. Much the same trend occurred a decade or two ago when insurance companies began reimbursing policyholders for psychiatric treatment and hospice care.

Reimbursement by insurance companies is "destiny," says medical-industry consultant Jerry Kantor. "Nothing in medicine is perceived as entirely legitimate until it's reimbursed. Acupuncturists suspect that for the profession, mandated . . . reimbursement would be more validating than a Nobel Prize awarded to an acupuncturist."[5]

Of course, a company must carefully weigh any decision to offer alternative-medicine benefits to its employees. For instance, such benefits could be costly for employers; in addition, the benefits could wind up being taxable as employee income.[6]

Then, too, the government could just as easily crack down on alternative-medicine practices as mandate that they be covered by insurance. As with trends in insurance coverage, issues of government regulation will go a long way toward determining the future of alternative medicine in the United States.

Some states have already set licensing standards for practitioners. This trend helps to legitimize alternative care. But it also limits who can practice alternative therapy and what standards of quality they must meet.

What is more, there is little uniformity to the regulation. That can lead to confusion among consumers, insurers, and medical providers trying to figure out what therapies are safe and useful.

For a look at the shifting regulatory scene, consider the information that David M. Sale, a lawyer, collected in a large-scale research project on laws affecting various forms of alternative practices.[7] For acupuncture alone, Sale's research pointed to a wide range of state laws and regulatory setups.

According to a report by Sale, six states had established acupuncture boards made up mainly of nonphysician acupuncturists; the boards were responsible for exercising independent regulatory authority over the acupuncture profession. In thirteen jurisdictions, a medical board applied administrative control over acupuncture, often with the help of an acupuncture board or committee. Eight states regulated the acupuncture profession above the board level within a state agency, usually with help from an acupuncture unit whose authority varied from state to state.

Some states defined acupuncture in terms of "traditional" Chinese or Eastern medical concepts, but other states used definitions that included modern Chinese or Eastern medical concepts or modern diagnostic techniques, Sale's report said.

Many feel that regulating the bewildering array of herbal remedies, like this selection in a Chinese shop, should be an important priority of the FDA. This would help give consumers the information they need to choose these remedies wisely.

"Depending on the state, practice rights may extend to medical doctors, osteopaths, chiropractors, physician assistants, naturopaths, homeopaths, podiatrists, nurses, veterinarians, and dentists," Sale noted.

Training requirements for other acupuncture practitioners also varied, and rules governing medical supervision of acupuncture practitioners were diverse, Sale found.

As alternative medicine becomes more and more popular, government officials will come under new pressure from consumer groups and the medical industry to set new standards for training and quality of care.

Nowhere will the pressure be stronger than on the makers of herbal products that make health claims. Many critics believe state and federal regulators should play a stronger role in regulating the huge supply of over-the-counter herbal and dietary-supplement products available to the public. But many regulators say they do not have the resources to do an effective job of overseeing the fast-growing alternative-medicine field. And industries that make and market herbal remedies are not likely to back down in the face of efforts to regulate their products.

For an example of how the competing forces of consumer watchdog groups, regulators, and industry representatives have wrestled with one another, consider the controversy over so-called functional foods—foods that contain herbal supplements and that manufacturers claim have health benefits.

In the summer of 2000, the Center for Science in the Public Interest, a consumer watchdog group in Washington, D.C., accused a variety of food manufacturers of selling products such as drinks and breakfast cereals that contained what the center said were "illegal" and potentially harmful ingredients. It issued 158 pages of complaints concerning more than 75 products and urged the Food and Drug Administration to put a stop to the sale of the foods.

Among the products singled out by the center was a tea drink containing kava kava that claimed to "enlighten" the senses. "Kava kava has been a factor in several arrests for driving while intoxicated," the center said. Another product billed as "mind enhancing" contained ginkgo biloba, which the center said "acts as a blood thinner. Taking ginkgo biloba with anticoagulant drugs may increase the risk of excessive bleeding or stroke."

"It's shameful that respected companies are selling modern-day snake oil," said Bruce Silverglade, director of legal affairs for the center.[8]

The group joined with the Connecticut attorney general and an expert on herbal medicine in attacking the foods.

For its part, the General Accounting Office, a part of the federal government that acts as a watchdog over other government agencies, said that the FDA's efforts to oversee "functional foods" had not been strong enough to ensure that the products were safe.[9]

The Grocery Manufacturers of America, an industry trade group, meanwhile staunchly defended the functional-food industry and said that brand-name companies sell safe products.[10]

The conflict over functional foods is part of a much larger set of issues that will no doubt take years to sort out as alternative therapies grow in prominence:

- When is a natural substance such as an herb a medicine, and when is it a food? When should it be regulated by the government as a medicine? Caffeine is a natural substance that has physical effects—should coffee and soft drinks with caffeine be treated as drugs? What about orange juice with extra calcium, or breakfast cereal with extra vitamins?

- Likewise, when is a treatment approach real medicine, and when is it pseudo medicine? Is a technique such as massage or aromatherapy a medical procedure? How much training should people be required to have before they can perform acupuncture, prescribe herbs, or teach *qigong*?

- And what of conventional Western medicine? It doesn't always work. Many treatments are experimental. Some prescription medications have dangerous side effects, just as alternative remedies sometimes do. Should Western and alternative treatments be held to the same scientific standards? Should alternative treatments be held to looser—or more rigorous—standards than those for conventional ones? Should insurance companies treat all therapies the same, or cover conventional ones more generously than alternative ones?

As alternative medicine grows and matures, and as our culture becomes more familiar with the huge array of alternative treatments, these are questions that policy makers, medical practitioners, and patients will have to consider carefully.

The best approach is always to be a smart consumer of medical services and, unless it is an emergency, to ask as many questions as possible before deciding on a treatment. After all, it is your health and safety that are most important.

SOURCE NOTES

Chapter One
1. "Unconventional Medicine in the United States," *The New England Journal of Medicine*, Jan. 28, 1993.
2. Study quoted in "Alternative Medicine Gains a Foothold," *The New York Times*, January 31, 2000, p. A1.
3. Larissa MacFarquhar, "Andrew Weil, Shaman, M.D.," *The New York Times Magazine*, August 24, 1997, p. 28.

Chapter Two
1. Michael Castleman, *The Healing Herbs: The Ultimate Guide to the Curative Power of Nature's Medicines.* (Emmaus, Pa.: Rodale Press, 1991), p. 9.
2. N.R. Farnsworth et. al., "Medicinal Plants in Therapy," *Bulletin of the World Health Organization* 63, no. 6 (1985).
3. Castleman, p. 1.

4. Jane E. Brody, "Taking Stock of Mysteries of Medicine," *The New York Times*, May 5, 1998, p. C7.
5. "The Mainstreaming of Alternative Medicine," *Consumer Reports*, May 2000, p. 17.
6. "Remembering Ginkgo & DHEA," Center for Science in the Public Interest, May 1998, Web site.
7. Denise Grady, "Scientists Say Herbs Need More Regulation," *The New York Times*, March 7, 2000, p. D1.
8. David Schardt, "Echinacea: Still Out in the Cold," *Nutrition Action Health Letter*, Center for Science in the Public Interest, April 1998, Web site.
9. Terence Monmaney, "Garlic Pills Called Useless for Cholesterol," *Los Angeles Times*, Washington Edition, June 17, 1998, p. 1.
10. Grady, *The New York Times*, op. cit.
11. Denise Grady, "Study Finds Herbal Remedy Useless Against Depression," *The New York Times*, April 18, 2001, p. A16.
12. Grady, "Scientists Say Herbs Need More Regulation."
13. Dan Vergano, "Study Shows St. John's Wort Might Weaken Birth Control," *USA Today*, May 1, 2000.
14. Emma Ross, "Two Studies Fault St. John's Wort," Associated Press.
15. Geoffrey Cowley and Anne Underwood, "What Is SAMe?" *Newsweek*, July 5, 1999.
16. "Dietary Supplements," *The CQ Researcher*, July 8, 1994.
17. Ibid.
18. Guy Gugliotta, "Ephedra Lawsuits Show Big Increase," *The Washington Post*, July 23, 2000.
19. Anne Woodham and Dr. David Peters, *Encyclopedia of Healing Therapies* (London: Dorling Kindersley, 1997), p. 62.
20. Isadora Stehlin, "Homeopathy: Real Medicine or Empty Promises?" *FDA Consumer* magazine, December 1996.
21. Dana Ullman, "Ten Most Frequently Asked Questions on Homeopathic Medicine," 1995, www.homeo-

pathic.com/intro/tenques.htm.

22. "Homeopathy," Microsoft Encarta Online Encyclopedia 2000.

23. Ibid.

24. Ibid.

25. From a position paper on homeopathy adopted in February 1994 by the National Council Against Health Fraud, the National Council for Reliable Health Information Web site, www.ncahf.org.

26. National Institutes of Health, National Center for Complementary and Alternative Medicine, Major Domains of Complementary & Alternative Medicine, http://nccam.nih.gov.

27. The Burton Goldberg Group, *Alternative Medicine: The Definitive Guide* (Tiburon, CA: Future Medicine Publishing Inc., 1997).

Chapter Three

1. Larry Dossey, "Spirituality, Healing, and the Soul," Center for Mind/Body Medicine: July 17, 1996.

2. Kenneth R. Pelletier, "Between Mind and Body: Stress, Emotions, and Health," *Mind/Body Medicine: How to Use Your Mind For Better Health*, Daniel Goleman and Joel Gurin, eds. (Yonkers, NY: Consumer Reports Books, 1993), pp. 19–38.

3. Bill Moyers, *Healing and the Mind* (New York: Doubleday, 1993), p. 239.

4. "Religion Today," Associated Press, Aug. 20, 1998.

5. Ibid.

6. Ibid.

7. Moyers, p. 225.

8. "Study Faults Faith Healing," *The New York Times*, April 7, 1998, p. C7.

9. Ibid, pp. 226, 227.

10. *The New England Journal of Medicine*, Dec. 6, 1979.

11. Martin L. Rossman, "Imagery: Learning to Use the Mind's Eye," in *Mind/Body Medicine: How to Use Your Mind For Better Health*, Daniel Goleman and Joel Gurin, eds. (Yonkers, NY: Consumer Reports Books, 1993), p. 291.

12. The Burton Goldberg Group, p. 75.
13. Herbert Benson, "The Relaxation Response," *Mind/Body Medicine: How to Use Your Mind For Better Health*, Daniel Goleman and Joel Gurin, eds. (Yonkers, NY: Consumer Reports Books, 1993), p. 236.

Chapter Four
1. Dr. Isadore Rosenfeld, MD, "Acupuncture Goes Mainstream (Almost)," *Parade*, August 16, 1998, p. 10.
2. Margalit Fox, "Read This or We'll Stick the Dog Again," *The New York Times*, April 12, 1998, p. 6.
3. Richard L. Worsnop, "Alternative Medicine's Next Phase," *The CQ Researcher*, Feb. 14, 1997, p. 128.
4. Richard A. Cooper and Sandi J. Stoflet, "Trends in the Education and Practice of Alternative Medicine Clinicians," *Health Affairs*, Fall 1996, p. 226.
5. Rick Weiss, "NIH Panel Endorses Acupuncture Therapy," *The Washington Post*, Nov. 6, 1997, p. 1.
6. Ibid.
7. Jane E. Brody, "U.S. Panel on Acupuncture Calls for Wider Acceptance," *The New York Times*, Nov. 6, 1997.
8. Rick Weiss, *The Washington Post*, op. cit.
9. Ibid.
10. Anne Woodham and Dr. David Peters, *Encyclopedia of Healing Therapies* (London: Dorling Kindersley, 1997), p. 91.
11. Ibid.
12. Weiss, *The Washington Post*, op cit.
13. The Burton Goldberg Group, p. 424.
14. William Collinge, The American Holistic Health Association Complete Guide to Alternative Medicine (New York: Warner Books, 1996), p. 283.
15. "Therapeutic Touch Fails to Detect 'Human Energy Field,'" *Science News Update*, Journal of the American Medical Association Web site.

16. Gina Kolata, "A Child's Paper Poses a Medical Challenge," *The New York Times*, April 1, 1998.
17. Ibid.
18. Linda Rosa, Emily Rosa, Larry Sarner, Stephen Barrett M.D., "A Close Look at Therapeutic Touch," *Journal of the American Medical Association*, April 1, 1998.
19. Kolata, *The New York Times*, op. cit.
20. Rosa, et. al., abstract on *Journal of the American Medical Association* Web site.
21. Kolata, *The New York Times*, op. cit.
22. Rosa, et. al, editor's note.
23. Ibid.

Chapter Five
1. Jerry Ackerman, "Alternative Medicine Goes Mainstream," *The Boston Globe*, April 12, 1998.
2. Landmark Healthcare Inc., *The Landmark Report II on HMOs and Alternative Care*, www.landmarkhealthcare.com/home.htm, 1999.
3. Laura Sullivan, "An Alternative Fit, Complementary and Alternative Medicine," *Risk Management*, April 1, 2000.
4. Lynna Goch, "Alternative Medicine Moves into the Mainstream," *Best's Review*, Life-Health Insurance Edition, March 1997, p. 84.
5. Ibid.
6. Sullivan, *Risk Management*, op.cit.
7. David M. Sale, "Overview of Legislative Development Concerning Alternative Health Care in the United States," a research project of the Fetzer Institute. www.healthy.net/public/legal-lg/regulations/fetzer.htm.
8. Center for Science in the Public Interest, "FDA Urged to Halt Sale of 'Functional Foods' Containing Illegal Ingredients," www.cspinet.org/new/fda_functfoods.html.
9. Ibid.
10. Lauran Neergaard, "Herbal Supplemented Food Criticized," Associated Press, July 18, 2000.

GLOSSARY

acupressure: The stimulation of blocked energy points using finger or hand pressure instead of acupuncture needles.

acupuncture: The insertion of hair-thin needles at strategic points of the body to block pain or restore health. According to traditional Chinese thought, acupuncture stimulates or disperses energy, or *chi*, that flows along invisible channels in the body.

applied kinesiology: A diagnostic technique that tests for imbalances in the body's systems by identifying weakness in particular muscles.

aromatherapy: A method of inhaling or applying to the skin essential oils extracted from plants to address physical or emotional disorders or induce relaxation.

ayurvedic medicine: A holistic approach developed in India more than five thousand years ago that combines the use of herbs, diet adjustments, exercise, massage, and meditation, among other techniques. Ayurveda, which means "science of life," teaches that health is the balance of five elements: air, earth, fire, ether, and water. The discipline is based on three basic biological forces in nature that shape one's "mind-body type." Those forces are seen in individual preferences, inclinations, and personal characteristics.

biofeedback: A method of learning to control bodily functions such as heart rate, blood pressure, and skin temperature using simple electronic monitoring devices.

chiropractic: A method of correcting misalignments in the bones of the spinal column to alleviate pressure on nerves that are connected to various tissues and organs.

electromyographic: A type of biofeedback sensor that, when attached to the body, shows electrical impulses that are associated with muscle response.

endorphins: Proteins in the brain that are associated with, among other things, the regulation and relief of pain.

energy therapy: A system that uses devices to measure the body's electromagnetic forces to detect imbalances that can signal disease or illness.

fibromyalgia: A medical condition in which a patient has pain and stiffness throughout the body.

guided imagery: A psychological technique for fighting stress and illness that employs the imagination to visualize positive outcomes to situations.

holistic medicine: A treatment approach in which the various systems of the body are seen as interdependent and parts of an integrated whole.

homeopathy: A system of medical treatment based on the idea that "like cures like." It uses minute doses of natural remedies to stimulate the body's natural defenses. In larger doses, the homeopathic remedies would cause illness.

hypnotherapy: A method of improving concentration, alertness, and relaxation using hypnosis, a state in which a patient becomes highly responsive to suggestion.

light therapy: A treatment that uses artificial light to treat depression and skin conditions.

magnetic-field therapy: A noninvasive treatment using magnets applied to specific areas of the body to treat broken bones, pain, and stress.

musculoskeletal: The system of the body that is made up of bones, cartilage, muscles, joints, and connective tissue.

music therapy: The use of music to treat psychological and physical illness, reduce stress, and aid people with disabilities.

naturopathy: A holistic approach to healing that relies on natural remedies, such as herbs, massage, diet, and lifestyle changes.

psychoneuroimmunology: A branch of research that deals with the way in which the brain can affect the body's immune responses.

qigong: A Chinese system that combines physical and breathing exercises with meditation to facilitate healing and wellness.

reflexology: A system of using finger pressure to stimulate nerve endings in the foot or hand to restore health to corresponding organs and body parts.

rolfing: A trademarked approach developed by biophysicist Ida Rolf that deals with the proper alignment of the head, torso, legs, and other parts of the body.

serotonin: A brain chemical that works as a kind of messenger, performing communication functions in the brain and body.

shiatsu: A massage technique that employs the system of points and meridians that acupuncture uses to affect the flow of *chi* in the body.

therapeutic touch: A technique in which a therapist attempts to rebalance a patient's energy field to restore health. The therapist places his or her hands a few inches above the patient's body and moves them over it to detect disruptions in the field.

yoga: Stretching, breathing, and meditation techniques designed to induce emotional and physical relaxation and tone the muscles.

RESOURCES

American Association of
Naturopathic Physicians
8201 Greensboro Drive
Suite 300
McLean, VA 22102
703-610-9005
www.naturopathic.org

American Association of
Oriental Medicine
433 Front Street
Catasauqua, PA 18032
Phone: 610-266-1433
Fax: 610-264-2768
www.aaom.org

American Chiropractic
Association
1701 Clarendon Boulevard
Arlington, VA 22209
800-986-4636
www.amerchiro.org

American Herbalists Guild
1931 Gaddia Road
Canton, GA 30115
770-751-6021
www.americanherbalists-
guild.com/main.htm

American Music Therapy
Association
8455 Colesville Road
Suite 1000
Silver Spring, MD 20910
301-589-3300
www.musictherapy.org

Association for Applied
Psychophysiology and
Biofeedback
10200 West 44th Avenue
Suite 304
Wheat Ridge, CO 80033-2840
303-422-8436
www.aapb.org

Center for Mind-Body
Medicine
5225 Connecticut Avenue NW
Suite 414
Washington, DC 20015
202-966-7338
www.nccam.nih.gov

Center for Science in the
Public Interest
1875 Connecticut Avenue,
NW
Suite 300
Washington, DC 20009
202-332-9110
www.cspinet.org

Food and Drug
Administration
www.fda.gov

National Center for
Homeopathy
801 North Fairfax
Suite 306
Alexandria, VA 22314
703-548-7790
homeopathic.org

National Guild of Hypnotists
P.O. Box 308
Merrimack, NH 03054-0308
603-429-9438
www.ngh.net

National Institutes of Health
National Center for
Complementary and
Alternative Medicine
PO Box 8218
Silver Spring, MD 20907-
8218
888-644-6226
altmed.od.nih.gov/oam

Quackwatch
www.quackwatch.com

FOR FURTHER READING

The Burton Goldberg Group, *Alternative Medicine: The Definitive Guide.* Tiburon, CA: Future Medicine Publishing, 1997.

This 1,000-plus-page book presents a highly favorable survey of the broad arena of alternative medicine. "Conventional medicine is superb when it comes to surgery, emergency, and trauma," Burton Goldberg writes. "But there's no question that alternative medicine works better for just about everything else." The volume, in which the publisher says "380 leading-edge physicians explain their treatments," covers more than 40 alternative therapies, from acupuncture to yoga. It also includes detailed chapters on health conditions and discussions of conventional and alternative treatments. In addition, there is a quick-reference guide to other medical problems. Included are details of historical and recent research on alternative therapies, plus discussion of the therapies' limitations and dangers and bibliographies and lists of organizations where further information is available.

Castleman, Michael. *The Healing Herbs: the Ultimate Guide to the Curative Power of Nature's Medicines*. Emmaus, PA: Rodale Press, 1991.

This book looks at 100 herbs, tracing their history and medicinal uses and explaining relevant scientific research on their benefits and hazards. Broken into easy-to-read chapters and sections, the volume includes a black-and-white drawing of each herb. It also offers a "fast-action guide" to various medical conditions, herbs that can be useful in treating them, and special precautions that users should take.

Check, William A. *The Mind-Body Connection*, in *The Encyclopedia of Health: Medical Disorders and Their Treatment*, ed. Dale C. Garell, M.D. New York: Chelsea House, 1990.

This slim volume offers a useful overview of the mind-body connection, including its history, the link between emotions and health, and the chemistry of emotions and behavior. The book also includes a useful glossary of terms, a roster of professional organizations, and a list of further readings.

Chevallier, Andrew. *The Encyclopedia of Medicinal Plants: A Practical Reference Guide to More Than 550 Key Medicinal Plants & Their Uses*. New York: DK Publishing, 1996.

Richly illustrated with color photos throughout, this coffee-table-size volume traces the development of herbal medicine from its early origins to its modern-day uses, and it offers a detailed visual and written guide to 100 key medicinal plants from around the world. In addition, it covers another 450 herbs, describing their therapeutic properties and uses. The volume also offers information on growing medicinal plants and consulting herbal practitioners, a listing of herbs by ailment, a glossary, and a short list of herbal suppliers, training courses, and professional groups.

Dossey, Larry. *Healing Words: The Power of Prayer and the Practice of Medicine.* San Francisco: Harper, 1993.
Dossey's pioneering work in the area of spirituality and healing is in this book. Its three sections—"Understanding Prayer and Healing," "Factors Influencing the Efficacy of Prayer," and "The Evidence"—explore such questions of where prayers go once they are said, an inquiry into how prayer can hurt, and an exploration of love and healing.

Dougans, Inge. *The Complete Illustrated Guide to Reflexology: Therapeutic Foot Massage for Health and Wellbeing.* Rockport, MA: Element Books, 1996.
Illustrated with color photos and diagrams, this book offers a thorough explanation of the art of therapeutic foot massage, from the history of "the foot in culture" to a look at how reflexology can help with problems of the nervous, circulatory, and endocrine systems, with pain, and even with terminal diseases. A reference section features a glossary, bibliography, and list of reflexology groups around the world.

Elias, Jason and Shelagh Ryan Masline. *The A to Z Guide to Healing Herbal Remedies.* New York: Dell Publishing, 1995.

This paperback volume covers more than 100 herbs and common ailments and includes a chapter on using herbs to maintain "optimum health and vitality." The "A to Z Guide" of healing herbs includes a brief summary of precautions for each.

Fischer-Rizzi, Susanne. *Complete Aromatherapy Handbook: Essential Oils for Radiant Health*. New York: Sterling Publishing, 1990.
A useful introduction to the field of aromatherapy, this illustrated book discusses more than two dozen essential oils, briefly explores the history of aromatherapy, and provides an overview of the methods used to extract the oils from plants. A "therapeutic index" lists a variety of illnesses and treatments.

Goleman, Daniel and Joel Gurin, eds. *Mind Body Medicine: How to Use Your Mind for Better Health*. Yonkers, NY: Consumer Reports Books, 1993.
Containing more than two dozen chapters written by scholars in mind-body medicine, this book ranges from the basics of this emerging discipline to discussions of the mind's role in illness and an exploration of how readers can help others cope with illness. A lengthy list of resources and reference materials is offered at the end of the book.

Hadady, Letha. *Asian Health Secrets: The Complete Guide to Asian Herbal Medicine*. New York: Crown Publishers, 1996.
More than an encyclopedia of herbal remedies, this volume offers a variety of diagnostic approaches based on traditional Asian medicine, from a section on "how to read your tongue" to one that shows how to determine a person's constitutional type through observation

of the hands. Subjects treated in the book include eating disorders, pain and injury, and the use of herbs to treat depression and improve memory and performance.

Loudon, Irvine, ed. *Western Medicine: An Illustrated History*. New York: Oxford University Press, 1997.

For those wanting to know about conventional Western medicine, this scholarly and richly illustrated book provides a thorough treatment, from Hippocrates to modern health care. A chapter titled "Unofficial and Unorthodox Medicine" by Margaret Pelling, deputy director of the Wellcome Unit for the History of Medicine at the University of Oxford, examines the long history of medical quackery and the characteristics of "official medicine." The book includes a useful chronology detailing nearly three thousand years of medical history.

Moyers, Bill. *Healing and the Mind*. New York: Doubleday, 1993.

The companion volume to an innovative Public Broadcasting System series on the mind-body connection, this book features interviews, in question-and-answer format, with some of the leading thinkers on medicine and the psyche. It addresses topics ranging from the brain and the immune system to the role that patients play in healing.

Reid, Daniel. *The Complete Book of Chinese Health and Healing*. Boston: Shambhala, 1994.

This authoritative volume covers traditional Chinese medicine from its theoretical roots to the "new medicine," which, the author says, "treats the human body as a balanced living organism in which all functions are mutually dependent, rather than a machine in which defective parts can be removed and replaced." Chapters exploring Chinese concepts of the body's energy pathways and the practice of *qigong* are especially useful.

Siegel, Bernie S. *Love, Medicine & Miracles.*
New York: Harper & Row, 1986.
This first-person exploration of the mind-body connection and healing presents a readable and anecdote-filled look at self-healing and the experiences of patients facing serious illness such as cancer.

The Drug & Natural Medicine Advisor, New
York: Time-Life Books, 1997.
A large compendium arranged in alphabetical order, this guide covers both alternative and conventional medications. It includes listings of brand-name and generic prescription drugs such as Prozac and Lanoxin (digoxin), herbal remedies such as ginkgo and rosemary, treatments such as calcium channel blockers, and a wide range of other therapies.

Woodham, Anne and Dr. David Peters.
Encyclopedia of Healing Therapies. New York:
DK Publishing, 1997.
This volume covers the gamut of alternative medicine, from touch and movement therapies such as acupressure and *t'ai chi ch'uan* to mind and emotion therapies like *feng shui* and light treatment. It also offers an index of treatment options for more than 200 health problems.

INDEX

Page numbers in *italics* refer to illustrations.

111